YOU AND

A Practical Guide to the Legal Rights and Responsibilities of Householders

by

RICHARD M. CHAPMAN
M.I.E.H., M.R.S.H., M.I.O.A., M.I.S.H.S.

Assistant Director of Environmental Health
Rotherham Metropolitan Borough Council

LONDON
Published by
SHAW & SONS LTD.,
Shaway House, SE26 5AE
1984

Published – – – May 1984
ISBN 07219 0990 6

Printed in Great Britain

To

KATHRYN

CONTENTS

PREFACE

Whether you are an owner-occupier, or tenant, or landlord you have rights and responsibilities with regard to your home or letting and its environment.

In this book, I have set out to enumerate the more commonly encountered laws with which conformity is due, and those enabling the householder to exercise his or her rights.

The introduction defines tenancies of all kinds, ownership, and what is meant by and included in your 'house' or 'premises'.

Part I deals with your legal rights, from tenure to grants, peaceful occupation, public services and appeals.

Part II considers your responsibilities in connection with nuisance, pets, pests, public services, access and liability, planning and building regulations.

The subject matter is necessarily wide, and where space has precluded exhaustive discussion, the footnote references will enable the reader to obtain further clarification, if required.

I have written this book as a comprehensive guide primarily for the householder, and where appropriate practical advice is given on making applications and appeals. The book will also fulfill the role of an *aide memoire* for property managers, Environmental Health Officers and others connected with enforcement of the statutes concerned. Additionally, the book will provide a work of quick reference for members of Local Authorities, citizens advisors, and the professional legal advisor who might find himself in less familiar territory.

I acknowledge with gratitude the assistance and contributions of many friends and associates in the compilation of this book.

I am indebted to Mr. Neil H. Morton, Director of Environmental Health, Rotherham M.B.C., for his encouragement and support. I am grateful to Mrs. N. D. Coupland for her punctilious approach to the English language, in her thorough perusal of the text. For help with the paragraphs on Electricity and Gas, I express my thanks to Mr. Christopher Burge and Mr. Brian Moss respectively.

In particular, I would like to thank Mr. Stephen Glossop, Legal Executive, for his indispensible proof reading and checking of the text. I am especially grateful to him for the paragraphs on County Court and High Court procedures in Chapter 6.

In a work of this kind, only the presentation and certain subject matter related to my own experience can claim to be original. If I have not detailed every reference from which material is drawn, it is because that material is firmly established as authoritative in the field, and the author is widely recognised.

Finally, I acknowledge the patience and understanding of my wife Kathryn, without which this book could not have been completed.

RICHARD M. CHAPMAN

WORKSOP
NOTTS.

March 1984

AN EXPLANATION OF THE FOOTNOTES

References to Acts of Parliament, Statutory Instruments and court cases are given in the footnotes for those readers who wish to refer to relevant sources.

Acts of Parliament which have been amended or modified may be noted by the phrase "as amended" Acts are given abbreviations of title and the year in which they received the Royal assent.

The full titles of these Acts and other abbreviations are given below:

Section or Sections of an Act	s. or ss.
Schedule to an Act or Statutory Instrument	... Schd.
Regulation of a Statutory Instrument ...	... Reg.

A.A. 1971	Animals Act 1971
A.A.A. 1960	Abandonment of Animals Act 1960
A.B.E.A. 1963 ...	Animal Boarding Establishments Act 1963
A.(C.P.)A. 1962	Animals (Cruel Poisons) Act 1962
A.H.A. 1981	Animal Health Act 1981
B.D.A. 1973	Breeding of Dogs Act 1973
B.T.A. 1981	British Telecommunications Act 1981
B.T.C.A. 1949 ...	British Transport Commission Act 1949
C.A. 1971	Courts Act 1971
C.A.A. 1956	Clean Air Act 1956
C.A.A. 1965	Clean Air Act 1965
C.L.A. 1977	Criminal Law Act 1977
C.P.A. 1974	Control of Pollution Act 1974
C.S.D.P.A. 1970	Chronically Sick and Disabled Persons Act 1970
D.A. 1871	Dogs Act 1871
D.A. 1906	Dogs Act 1906

D.(A)A. 1928	Dogs (Amendment) Act 1928
D.(A)A. 1938	Dogs (Amendment) Act 1938
D.L.A. 1957	Dog Licenses Act 1957
D.P.A. 1972	Defective Premises Act 1972
D.W.A.A. 1976	Dangerous Wild Animals Act 1976
E.A. 1944	Education Act 1944
E.A. 1947	Electricity Act 1947
E.A. 1957	Electricity Act 1957
E.L.A. 1882	Electric Lighting Act 1882
E.L.A. 1909	Electric Lighting Act 1909
E.L.(C)A. 1899	Electric Lighting (Clauses) Act 1899
E.(S)A. 1882–1936	Electricity (Supply) Acts 1882–1936
G.A. 1972	Gas Act 1972
G.A. 1980	Gas Act 1980
G.C.A. 1847	Gasworks Clauses Act 1847
G.D.A. 1975	Guard Dogs Act 1975
G.R.A. 1967	General Rating Act 1967
H.A. 1949	Housing Act 1949
H.A. 1957	Housing Act 1957
H.A. 1961	Housing Act 1961
H.A. 1964	Housing Act 1964
H.A. 1969	Housing Act 1969
H.A. 1974	Housing Act 1974
H.A. 1980	Housing Act 1980
H.F.A. 1972	Housing Finance Act 1972
H.(H.P.)A. 1977	Housing (Homeless Persons) Act 1977
H.I.A. 1978	Homes Insulation Act 1978
H.S.W.A. 1974	Health and Safety at Work Act 1974
H.W.A. 1980	Highways Act 1980
L.A. 1983	Litter Act 1983
L.C.A. 1961	Land Compensation Act 1961
L.C.A. 1973	Land Compensation Act 1973
L.D.A. 1976	Land Drainage Act 1976
L.G.A. 1972	Local Government Act 1972
L.G.A. 1974	Local Government Act 1974
L.G.(M.P.)A. 1976	Local Government (Miscellaneous Provisions) Act 1976
L.G.(M.P.)A. 1982	Local Government (Miscellaneous Provisions) Act 1982
L.G.(P.L.)A. 1980	Local Government (Planning and Land) Act 1980
L.P.A. 1925	Law of Property Act 1925
L.P.A. 1969	Law of Property Act 1969

L.R.A. 1967 ... ... Leasehold Reform Act 1967
L.T.A. 1949 ... ... Landlord and Tenant Act 1949
L.T.A. 1962 ... ... Landlord and Tenant Act 1962
M.A. 1958 ... ... Manoeuvres Act 1958
M.Q.A. 1954 ... ... Mines and Quarries Act 1954
N.A.A. 1948 ... ... National Assistance Act 1948
O.L.A. 1957 ... ... Occupiers Liability Act 1957
P.A. 1832 ... ... Prescription Act 1832
P.A. 1911 ... ... Perjury Act 1911
P.A. 1954 ... ... Pests Act 1954
P.A.A. 1911 ... ... Protection of Animals Act 1911
P.A.(A)A. 1954 ... ...
Protection of Animals (Anaesthetics) Act 1954
P.A.(C.D.)A. 1933 ... ...
Protection of Animals (Cruelty to Dogs) Act 1933
P.D.P.A. 1949 ... Prevention of Damage by Pests Act 1949
P.F.E.A. 1977 ... ... Protection from Eviction Act 1977
P.H.A. 1875 ... ... Public Health Act 1875
P.H.A. 1936 ... ... Public Health Act 1936
P.H.A. 1961 ... ... Public Health Act 1961
P.H.(R.N.)A. 1969 ... ...
Public Health (Recurring Nuisances) Act 1969
P.O.A. 1953 ... ... Post Office Act 1953
P.O.A. 1969 ... ... Post Office Act 1969
R.A. 1967 ... ... Rent Act 1967
R.E.(G.A.E.B.)A. 1954 ... ...
Rights of Entry (Gas and Electricity Boards) Act 1954
R.L.A. 1959 ... ... Rights of Light Act 1959
R.T.A. 1972 ... ... Road Traffic Act 1972
T.A. 1968 ... ... Theft Act 1968
T.C.P.A. 1971 ... Town and Country Planning Act 1971
T.G.P.A. 1863 ... ... Town Gardens Protection Act 1863
T.I.A. 1971 ... ... Tribunals and Inquiries Act 1971
T.P.C.A. 1847 ... ... Town Police Clauses Act 1847
U.C.T.A. 1977 ... ... Unfair Contract Terms Act 1977
W.A. 1945 ... ... Water Act 1945
W.A. 1948 ... ... Water Act 1948
W.A. 1959 ... ... Water Act 1959
W.A. 1981 ... ... Water Act 1981
W.A. 1983 ... ... Water Act 1983
W.(P.I.)P.A. 1892 ... ...
Witnesses (Public Inquiries) Protection Act 1892

INTRODUCTION

Being the owner-occupier, tenant or landlord of a house or flat would seem to be a straightforward state of affairs, which for the most part it is. It becomes necessary, however, for you to know the extent of your **premises** or **land**, and what may be included as part of your **house**, when your rights and responsibilities as an owner and/or occupier are examined.

Your security of tenure will vary with the nature of your ownership or tenancy, and whether or not your property is security for a loan.

For these reasons it is necessary to give several definitions, which for the sake of accuracy, cannot readily be edited to remove dated expressions and verbal extravagance. References to "appurtenances" "messuages" and "hereditements" are to be found though the required explanations are given in the footnotes.

house—means a dwellinghouse, whether a private dwellinghouse or not,[1] and includes any yard, garden, outhouses and appurtenances[2] belonging thereto, or usually enjoyed therewith, and may also include any part of a building which is occupied or intended to be occupied as a separate dwelling.[3]

house, **dwelling-house** and **flat** are further defined though primarily for the purposes of the "right to buy".[4]

---

[1] P.H.A. 1936, s. 343 (1).
[2] belongings, appendages (*e.g.* an extension)
[3] H.A. 1957, s. 189 (1).
[4] H.A. 1980, s. 3—see Chapter 1, Para D, p. 13.

house in multiple occupation—a house which is occupied by persons who do not form a single household.[1] A house in which the rooms have been apportioned for separate exclusive occupation, with shared washing and cooking facilities would be in multiple occupation.

premises—includes messuages[2], buildings, lands, easements[3] and hereditaments[4] of any tenure.[5]

land—includes land covered by water, and any interest or right in, over or under land.[6]

residential occupier—in relation to any premises means a person occupying the premises as a residence, whether under a contract, or by virtue of any enactment or rule of law giving him the right to remain in occupation or restricting the right of any other person to recover possession of the premises.[7]

owner—in relation to any land, place or premises means a person who either on his own account or as agent or trustee for another person, is receiving the rackrent[8] of the land, place or premises, or would be entitled to receive it if the land, place or premises were let at a rackrent, and "owned" shall be construed accordingly.[9]

lease, lessor and lessee—the lease is the contract by which land or tenament is conveyed for a term by its owner (lessor) to a tenant (lessee) for a rent.

mortgage, mortgagee and mortgagor—the mortgage is the conveyance of property as security for debt, with provision for reconveyance by the lender (mortgagee) to the borrower (mortgagor) on payment of the debt within an agreed period.

---

[1] H.A. 1969, s. 58.
[2] dwelling-houses with outbuildings and land.
[3] Includes rights of way over anothers' ground, and any supplementary buildings.
[4] Properties and inheritances.
[5] P.H.A. 1936, s. 343 (1).
[6] H.A. 1980, s. 329(1).
[7] P.F.E.A. 1977, s. 1(1).
[8] Briefly, a rent greater than two thirds of the rateable value.
[9] L.G.(M.P.)A. 1976 s. 44(1).

tenant—(in general terms) a person having a right granted to him or any predecessor in title of his by a contract, or conferred by an enactment to occupy any premises as a residence in consideration of a rent. . . .[1]

regulated tenancy[2]—a letting by a non-residential private landlord, of furnished or unfurnished accommodation, which may be all or part of a house, flat, maisonnette or bungalow.

assured tenancy—a tenancy of newly built accommodation, usually provided by a building society, pension fund or insurance company which has been approved for the purpose of providing homes by the Secretary of State, Department of the Environment.[3]

Building work must have started after 8th August, 1980, and the property cannot have been previously occupied under any other form of tenancy.

protected shorthold tenancy—a form of regulated tenancy of any type of dwelling, granted for a fixed period of from one to five years.

Such a tenancy can only have been created after 28th November, 1980.[4]

secure tenancy—a letting of residential accommodation by either a local council; housing association, etc.[5] to an individual who occupies it as his or her principal home. The tenancy is either for a fixed term or period, and secure tenants have the right to buy[6] their homes, subject to certain qualifying conditions.

---

[1] L.T.A. 1962, s. 1(1).

[2] The Housing Act, 1980, s. 64(1), converted all former controlled tenancies (with rents based on 1956 rateable values) to regulated tenancies. Regulated tenancies may be either protected or statutory. A protected tenant has security by virtue of his contract with the landlord, and a statutory tenant has security under the Rent Acts.

[3] H.A. 1980, s. 56(4).

[4] H.A. 1980, operative date of s. 51.

[5] By H.A. 1980, s. 28(2), (4) also includes a County Council; the Commission for New Towns; a Development Corporation; the Housing Corporation; a Charitable Housing Trust; the Development Board for Rural Wales and certain Housing Associations.

[6] H.A. 1980, s. 1(1) see also Chapter 1, Para D, p. 13.

housing association tenancy—a secure tenancy (with some exceptions) granted to tenants of houses or flats which can broadly be described as self-contained, and are occupied as the only or principal residence.

The right to buy exists except for tenants of charitable housing associations or trusts.[1]

landlord—in relation to any premises occupied by a tenant under a right granted by a contract means the person who granted that right or any successor in title of his, as the case may require, in relation to any premises occupied by a tenant under a right conferred by an enactment, means the person who apart from that right, would be entitled to possession of the premises.[2]

ground landlord—an owner of land which is leased to someone at a ground rent.

---

[1] H.A. 1980, s. 2(1), (2).
[2] L.T.A. 1962, s. 6(1).

PART I

THE LEGAL RIGHTS OF HOUSEHOLDERS

CHAPTER 1

TENURE

A. SECURITY OF TENURE

"A man's house is his castle"[1] and many conflicts can be cited, where that state of affairs has been threatened, resulting in righteous or unrighteous indignation from the occupier. Possession in law consists of certain rights which arise when you assume control of premises with the intent to exclude others.

If you own the freehold of your property, then in principle you may exercise in it acts of ownership of all kinds,[2] subject of course to the many legal obligations enumerated in Part II.

As a residential occupier of rented accommodation, both you and members of your household are protected from unlawful eviction and harassment.[3] You are entitled to peace and comfort and to maintenance of the services

[1] Sir Edward Coke, 1552-1634, *Institutes: Commentary upon Littleton*.
[2] *Halsbury's Laws of England*, 3rd. Ed., Vol. 32, para 267.
[3] P.F.E.A. 1977, s. 1.

reasonably required for your occupation. Anyone who interferes with those rights, with the intention of depriving you of your occupation or preventing you from exercising any right or remedy, commits an offence.

When you buy the freehold of a house, you acquire ownership of it for an unlimited period. This ownership, however, is not strictly absolute, since no freehold property is completely safeguarded against compulsory purchase.[1]

If you let your home, or any part of it, on anything other than a protected shorthold or restricted contract[2] letting, you may prejudice your right to recover sole possession for some considerable time.

Your property may also be placed under a control order by the local council, if in multi-occupation and not provided with adequate facilities, means of escape in case of fire and not in good repair. The control order gives the council full powers of a mortgagee, to collect rents; carry out repairs and improvements, and create tenancies.

If your property is uninsured or underinsured you may sustain a major or complete loss in the event of severe damage through fire or subsidence.

As a tenant, you are assured, depending on the nature of your tenancy, unlimited occupation, provided that the rent, rates and other agreed charges are paid and the tenancy agreement is adhered to. As the tenant of a restricted contract or shorthold letting your occupancy can be brought to an end on the terms agreed when the letting commenced. A licensee, as opposed to a tenant, has less protection under the law. In the context of your home a lodger is an example of a licensee. If the lodger refuses to leave your home when requested, then although you are not obliged to serve a notice to quit, you must obtain a possession order from the County Court. Indeed persons who occupy property as squatters cannot lawfully be evicted without a court order.

---

[1] See, Para C., *below*, p. 9.

[2] Restricted contracts are mostly lettings where the landlord and tenant live in the same house or flat.

The distinction between a licence and a tenancy is not always straightforward and legal advice should be sought if in doubt.

You may be an owner-occupier of property which is subject to a mortgage. If you default in your payments, you can expect the building society or other mortgagee to commence proceedings to obtain a possession order. In practise mortgagees are generally helpful in such circumstances and the rules of building societies usually contain paragraphs entitled 'relief to mortgagors'. In order to assist a client, the mortgagee can suspend or vary the payment of principal or interest, or extend the period of the loan over which the balance is to be paid, at his discretion.

Notice to Quit

With the exceptions already mentioned, you cannot be evicted by a landlord or mortgagee unless he obtains a possession order. The county court may grant a suspended possession order, if satisfied that there is some prospect of the defaulter paying "the arrears within a reasonable time."

Whether or not a mortgagee would seek to dispossess you would depend, amongst other things, on the amount of the outstanding debt in relation to the principal already paid. If a mortgage is nearing the end of its term, then the mortgagee may seek to recover an outstanding sum by default action in the county court.[1]

In order for a landlord to obtain possession, he must establish that one of the grounds for possession set out in the Rent Act[2] applies. Whether or not a notice to quit is required depends in the main on the term of the tenancy. If it is a periodic tenancy—weekly or monthly with no end date fixed, then notice to quit is required. If a tenancy is fixed term—granted for definite periods, then it ends automatically when the agreed period of the tenancy runs out, and no notice to quit is needed.[3]

---

[1] An action to recover a sum of money.
[2] R.A. 1977, Schd. 15, Part 1.
[3] Includes: statutory, protected shorthold tenancies and lettings under licence.

In order to be valid, a notice to quit must be in writing; be given at least four weeks before it runs out, and include information relating to the landlord's right to seek an order for possession from the court when the notice expires, together with advice on seeking legal assistance.

Possession Order

In respect or periodic tenancies,[1] the grounds for possession are of two kinds. Those which are discretionary[2] upon the county court, and those cases which are mandatory.[3] The discretionary cases broadly follow and involve breaches of tenancy conditions, whilst the mandatory cases give no discretion to the court, and effectively involve temporary or shorthold tenancies. For the mandatory cases to apply, the tenant must have been notified in writing at the commencement of the tenancy, that the landlord may in future apply for possession on one of the stated grounds. When possession is actually required, the conditions of the appropriate mandatory case must be fulfilled.

Secure Tenancies

There are different rules for obtaining possession of your house if you are a local council or housing association tenant.

A tenancy granted by a private landlord will usually end when the notice to quit expires, and possession would be determined by the County Court. The landlord would cease to collect any rent for fear of creating a new tenancy although theoretically the tenant must still make a reasonable attempt to pay the rent, until the County Court determines the question of possession.

Under a secure tenancy, the grounds for possession[4] broadly follow those of the Rent Acts, but unlike a Rent Act tenancy, the secure tenancy does not end on termination of

---

[1] Includes: regulated, assured, secure, housing association and restricted contract tenancies.

[2] Cases 1–10, Schd. 15.

[3] Cases 11–20, Schd. 15.

[4] HA 1980, Schd. 4, part 1.

the notice to quit. A fixed term secure tenancy does not come to an end by the effluxion of time, and the landlord does not have a right to possession. The tenancy reverts to a periodic tenancy equivalent to a Rent Act 'statutory' tenancy.

Preliminary Notice

The County Court will not consider any application for possession, unless the council has served you with a preliminary notice in the prescribed form,[1] stating the grounds on which they will apply to the Court.[2]

In the case of a periodic tenancy, which most are, the notice must give a date after which possession proceedings will be commenced.[3] The notice expires after twelve months, and no proceedings can be brought after that time for possession, unless a new notice is served.

There are two overriding conditions to be satisfied in relation to the grounds for possession, and either or both may apply:[4]

(*a*) It must be reasonable to make the order in the circumstances existing at the time of the hearing. (The burden of proof is on the landlord)

(*b*) In certain cases, the Court will need to be satisfied that suitable alternative accommodation is available for you when the possession order takes effect.

B.—COVENANTS AND AGREEMENTS

Restrictions on how your property can be used or altered, may be written into the title deeds. They are known as **restrictive covenants**, and are binding on each new owner every time the property changes hands. They may prevent you from using your home for business purposes, or for any use other than as a private dwelling. They may prohibit the

---

[1] HA 1980, s. 33(1).
[2] HA 1980, s. 33(2).
[3] HA 1980, s. 33(3), (4).
[4] HA 1980, s. 34(2), (3).

erection of any other buildings, or the fencing of a front lawn or garden on an open plan estate.

If you find that a restrictive covenant is preventing you from concluding the sale, or hindering the use of your property, you may apply to the Lands Tribunal[1] to have it waived.

An **implied covenant** exists between landlord and tenant covering such matters as your obligation to pay rent, rates and insurance cover, and the landlord's duty to maintain the property in a state fit for human habitation, also guaranteeing the tenants lawful possession.

An **express covenant** is, however, in writing and is concerned with specific conditions written into a lease or agreement. A **full repairing lease** would clearly place the tenant or lessor under an obligation for all maintenance and repairs.

Mortgage deeds and leasing documents normally provide that on breach of a covenant or agreement in it, by the mortgagor or tenant, then the mortgagee or landlord may forfeit the tenancy and retake possession. You cannot however be summarily dispossessed, and the mortgagee or landlord must first serve notice, giving you the opportunity to rectify the specified breach and pay compensation, within a reasonable time.[2] If you consider that, for example, the time limit during which the breach is to be remedied is unreasonably short, then you can appeal to the county court.[3] As an alternative to possession proceedings and depending on who is in breach of a covenant, either party may sue for damages in the county court. The court may order the defendant to fulfil his or her obligations.

In general terms, an easement is right to use the land of another person for a certain purpose. You may wish to grant owners of neighbouring land rights of way over your property, or give permission for a connection to be made

[1] See Chapter 5, Para H, p. 100.

[2] L.P.A. 1925, s. 146. But no notice is required where possession is sought for non-payment of mortgage or rent.

[3] See Chapter 5, para C. p. 83.

into your private sewer,[1] and vice versa. It is customary for the person(s) requesting the easement to pay all legal costs, as well as agreeing with you a suitable payment for the easement.

Instead of an easement being expressly granted, you may acquire an easement by prescription, if you have enjoyed the uninterrupted use of land for more than twenty years. If the owner of the land fails to take any action to defeat your claim within that period, his remedy to restore his exclusive rights over his land may be lost.[2]

C. COMPULSORY PURCHASE AND COMPENSATION

Your house, whether tenanted or owner-occupied, may be compulsorily purchased by Order of the local district or county council in exercise of their powers under a variety of statutory rules:

(*a*) in conjunction with a clearance area, as part of a scheme for the provision of new housing.[3]

(*b*) for improvement in a Housing Action Area.[4]

(*c*) a 'listed building'[5] in need of repair.[6]

(*d*) for new roads or road widening.[7]

(*e*) for provision of local council facilities or services.[8]

With regard to housing matters, the local council must make a Compulsory Purchase Order (CPO), which requires confirmation by the Secretary of State, Department of the Environment before it can be put into operation. They must also serve notice on all owners, lessees and occupiers,[9] stating the effect of the Order; that it is about to be

---

[1] A sewer which is not a public sewer. P.H.A. 1936 s. 343.
[2] L.P.A. 1969.
[3] H.A. 1957. ss. 43, 51, and Schd. 3.
[4] H.A. 1974, s. 43.
[5] A building of historical or architectural interest.
[6] T.C.P.A. 1971, Part 6.
[7] H.W.A. 1980, Part 12.
[8] L.G.A. 1972, as amended and substituted by L.G.(P & L) A. 1980, Schd. 23.
[9] Except tenants for a month or less.

submitted for confirmation, and the period and manner in which objections may be made.

If you receive a notice of this kind, and wish to object, you should write to the Secretary of State at the address given, explaining why you think the council should not acquire your property.

For example, in respect of (*a*) above, you may consider that your house has been wrongly described as being "unfit for human habitation", and should either be excluded from the Order, or payment of compensation should represent current market value as opposed to site value only.

Where the "fitness" of your property is in dispute, the council must send you a "principal grounds notice" if you have objected to the Order. The notice lists the faults which, in the opinion of the council, render your house unfit, and must be sent to you at least 28 days before any public inquiry.

Unfit houses are shown on the map which accompanies the CPO, and are coloured pink. ("the pink properties") Houses which are not unfit, and other areas of land required by the council to make up a useable parcel of land, are coloured grey. ("the grey properties"). A house found by the public inquiry not to be unfit, will not necessarily be excluded from the Order, but changed from "pink" to "grey" property, where current market value is due to the owner.

You may in addition, make representations with respect to "well-maintained payments", if you have received a "well-maintained notification". In spite of any inherent structural defects or bad arrangement, you may consider that your house has been kept in a good state of repair and condition, contrary to the view of the council.

Where objections are raised on matters other than valuation,[1] the Secretary of State may order a local public inquiry.[2]

---

[1] Which are referred ultimately to the Lands Tribunal.

[2] See Chapter 5, para E. p. 92.

If you are permanently displaced due to compulsory purchase, you have a right to be provided with suitable alternative accommodation on reasonable terms.[1]

There are two principal grounds on which you can contest a **confirmed** CPO:

(*a*) that the council has selected the wrong power or it is using a valid power to achieve some improper purpose.

(*b*) that there has been some procedural irregularity.

Purchase on Demand of Owner

Circumstances may arise when you would wish your property to be purchased, and the law provides that the council must purchase where:

(*a*) following service on you of an Improvement Notice,[2] you serve a counter "purchase" notice.[3]

(*b*) where you are effectively prevented from selling your house due to public knowledge of impending re-development, you serve a "blight"[4] notice on the council.

If you wish your house to be purchased for one of the above reasons, the procedural steps to be followed include: service of a "blight" or "purchase" notice; negotiations for sale of the freehold, compensation etc; appeals to the Lands Tribunal[5] where necessary; conveyance of title to the council and re-housing.

Compensation

Landlords, tenants and owner-occupiers may be eligible for two forms of compensation; a payment in respect of the

---

[1] L.C.A. 1973, s. 39 as amended.

[2] H.A. 1974, ss. 88(1), 89(5). Notice to landlord to improve tenanted property.

[3] H.A. 1974, s. 101. Must be served within 6 months of receipt of an Improvement Notice.

[4] T.C.P.A. 1971, Part 9, as amended. You must first establish that you have attempted and failed to sell at a reasonable price on the open market. (s. 193)

[5] See Chapter 5, para H, p. 100.

property value, and a disturbance payment. Compensation for loss of your property is based on two fundamental assumptions: first that the owner should be paid current market value of the purchased property, and second that unfit[1] houses are worthless, the owner being entitled to site value only.

Current market value is the value the property would be expected to realise if offered by a willing seller on the open market, ignoring depreciation due to anticipated compulsory purchase, but taking into account any appreciation of site value due to its development potential in the absence of a CPO.[2]

A **well-maintained payment**[3] may be made to a landlord tenant or owner-occupier in respect of a house which although unfit, has been well cared for. Applications must be made within three months of the notice to treat or closing order.[4]

If you are displaced by a CPO, then you may be eligible for a **home loss payment**[5] which is intended to compensate households of sufficient longevity of occupation for the loss of an established home. The conditions of application are that the premises are vacated after the CPO is approved and that the claim is made within six months before or after the date of displacement. Local councils may make an equivalent payment to owners who voluntarily sell property where a CPO might have been made.[6] However, owners who serve a blight notice requiring the council to purchase are not eligible for a home loss payment.[7]

The amount of home loss payment you would receive is statutorily fixed, and is currently either £150, or three times

[1] H.A. 1957, s. 4—a house so far defective as to be not reasonably suitable for occupation.

[2] L.C.A. 1961, ss. 6, 9.

[3] A sum equal to eight times the rateable value, provided that site value and well maintained payment do not exceed market valuation.

[4] H.A. 1957, s. 17(1), 30(1).

[5] L.C.A. 1973, s. 29 as amended. Applies to owner occupiers and tenants covered by the Rent Acts, and service tenants of at least five years standing.

[6] L.C.A. 1973, s. 32(7).

[7] L.C.A. 1973, s. 29(5).

the rateable value of the house, up to a maximum of £1500, whichever is the greater.[1]

A **disturbance payment** is payable to any household permanently displaced as a result of a CPO, and amounts to the reasonable expenses of moving from the house.[2] There are no residency requirements as for home loss payments, but the property must be in lawful occupation. If you are entitled to receive full compensation at current market value, then you would not be eligible for a disturbance payment, as a similar sum would be included as part of the overall award. If agreement cannot be reached on the amount of disturbance payment between you and the council, then you are entitled to appeal to the Lands Tribunal.[3]

D. THE RIGHT TO BUY AND THE RIGHT TO A MORTGAGE

A significant feature of the Tenants Charter[4] is the right for **secure tenants**[5] to purchase the freehold or a long lease of their house or flat. If you are a tenant of a local council, new town or non-charitable housing association, and your tenancy has existed for three years (not necessarily in the same house) then you have the right to buy either on your own behalf; jointly with members of your family, or retain an option to buy at a fixed price within two years.[6]

You are entitled to a discount off the valuation of thirty-three percent after three years occupation, rising by one percent for each additional year, up to a maximum of fifty percent.[7]

---

[1] L.C.A. 1973, s. 30.
[2] L.C.A. 1973, s. 37(1).
[3] See Chapter 5 para H. p. 100.
[4] See para E. *below*, p. 16.
[5] See definitions in Introduction, p. xxi.
[6] H.A. 1980, Part 1.
[7] There are proposals in the Housing and Building Control Bill, to reduce the residency requirement to two years; increase the maximum discount to 60%, and extend the right to buy to secure tenants of charitable housing associations, and houses originally provided for persons of pensionable age.

For the purposes of the right to buy, "house", "dwelling-house" and "flat" are defined as follows:—a dwelling-house is a house if . . . it is a structure reasonably so called, so that:

(*a*) where a building is divided horizontally, the flats or other units into which it is divided are not houses, **and**

(*b*) where a building is divided vertically the units into which it is divided may be houses; **and**

(*c*) where a building is not structurally detached it is not a house if a material part of it lies above or below the remainder of the structure.[1] Any dwelling-house which is not a house, is a flat.[2]

The main exclusions from the right to buy, assuming you qualify as a secure tenant involve particular types of dwelling:

(*a*) "sheltered" dwellings for pensioners.

(*b*) dwellings specially adapted and designed for persons of pensionable age, to whom the landlord habitually grants tenancies.

(*c*) dwellings designed or specially adapted for the disabled.

In all the above cases you do not have the right to buy but the landlord may allow you to do so if he wishes.

The procedure for exercising your right to buy varies slightly depending on whether your landlord is a local council, new town or housing association.

As a council or new town tenant, you must complete and send to the council a right to buy **claim form**.[3] The landlord will reply with a **response notice** telling you whether or not your claim is valid. The landlord will then send you an

---

[1] Presumably an inter-locked house, though the overlap must be a **material** part of it.

[2] H.A. 1980, s. 3(1) summarised.

[3] Form RTB 1.

offer notice informing you of his valuation (and the right to contest it); your discount; the net purchase price; conditions of sale and details of your right to a mortgage. He will also send you a **mortgage notice**, for completion if you wish the landlord to arrange the finance. Your landlord should then reply with a **mortgage response**, informing you of the amount of mortgage to which you are entitled.

You may of course approach any building society, bank etc. for the necessary mortgage, and it is always desirable to seek legal advice when purchasing property. You will be expected to bear the cost of survey, search, conveyancing, land registration and stamp duty fees.

On agreement of mortgage and other matters of sale between you and the landlord, the purchase may be completed. The landlord may require you to complete within twenty-eight days unless you have claimed an option to purchase within two years.

If you are a tenant of a non-charitable housing association, the procedure is almost identical, except that the Housing Corporation with whom the association must be registered, provide the mortgage.

If you pay a ground rent, you will have the right to buy the freehold or extend the lease for fifty years,[1] if the following conditions are met:

(*a*) your lease was originally granted for more than twenty-one years, **and**

(*b*) your lease is of the whole house, **and**

(*c*) your lease is at a low rent,[2] **and**

(*d*) it is your only or main residence, and has been for the last three years, **and**

---

[1] L.R.A. 1967, as amended by H.A. 1969, s. 82; H.A. 1974, s. 118 and H.A. 1980, ss. 141, 142.

[2] Annual rent to be less than two-thirds of the rateable value, as assessed on 23rd March, 1965, or on the first day of the lease if granted after that date.

(*e*) the rateable value of your house was at one time within certain limits.[1]

You therefore have the choice between purchase of the freehold, extending the lease by 50 years or becoming a statutory tenant when your lease expires. Once a statutory tenant under the Rent Acts, you are liable to pay a fair rent as assessed by the rent officer.

The procedures for exercising your right to buy are as follows: you first serve notice of enfranchisement[2] or extension on your landlord, to which the landlord must reply within two months;[3] agree the price;[4] arrange the finance and agree the conditions of sale or extension; sign and exchange contracts.

In addition to bearing your own survey, land registration stamp duty and legal fees, you are also liable for the landlord's reasonable costs arising out of your notice which may include solicitors' conveyancing fees, valuers' fees etc.

Once having served a notice of enfranchisement, both parties are bound to implement it, except where the price was fixed before the notice was served, or determined by the Leasehold Valuation Tribunal, when you have one month to withdraw the notice.

E. TENANCY AGREEMENTS AND TENANTS' ASSOCIATIONS

Your tenancy agreement is drawn from the relevant statutory provisions[5] and the express terms of any written or oral agreement. The scope of tenancy agreements varies widely, and may be in the form of concise notes on the rear of a

[1] Further information: *Leasehold Reform*, Housing Booklet No. 9, Department of the Environment/Welsh Office. H.M.S.O.

[2] In the prescribed form. Leasehold Reform (Notices) Regulations 1967 and 1969 (S.I. 1967 No. 1768 and 1969 No. 1418.)

[3] Leasehold Reform (Enfranchisement and Extension) Regulations 1967, (S.I. 1967 No. 1879.)

[4] If not agreed, you may appeal to your local Leasehold Valuation Tribunal to fix the price.

[5] Landlord and Tenant, Protection from Eviction, Public Health and Housing Acts, etc.

pre-printed rent card[1], or a comprehensive document giving the obligations of both parties in detail, for which a tenant may be asked to sign an acceptance.

A tenancy agreement might include the following:

Rights and Responsibilities of the Tenant

Use of the Dwelling

(*a*) The tenant to use the dwelling as his or her principal home.

(*b*) Conditions as to lodgers; sub-letting and transfer of tenancy.

(*c*) Regulations concerning use of the dwelling so as not to cause nuisance, or establish in it any trade or business.

(*d*) Control of vehicle parking.

Payment of Rent

(*a*) Rent, rates and any other charges to be paid regularly and promptly. (weekly, monthly, in advance etc.)

(*b*) Landlord's right to change rent or other charges after giving four weeks notice; alterations to rates element without such notice.

Repairs and Maintenance

(*a*) Tenant to keep the dwelling in a clean and orderly condition.

(*b*) Tenant to inform landlord of any repairs required.

(*c*) Tenant to make good any damage due to misuse or neglect.

(*d*) Landlord's right to enter premises to make good any such damage and charge the tenant accordingly.

---

[1] The information to be contained is prescribed by The Rent Book (Forms of Notice) Regulations, 1982. (S.I. 1982, No. 1474) which apply to "restricted contract", "protected", and "statutory" tenancies.

(*e*) Tenant to leave the dwelling in a reasonable condition at the end of the tenancy.

Exterior Decorations and Improvements

(*a*) Tenant's rights to decorate outside of dwelling.

(*b*) Tenant's rights to make structural alterations or additions, for which landlord cannot unreasonably refuse permission.

(*c*) Tenant to obtain any necessary Building Regulations approval or Planning Permission in connection with (*b*) above.

The Right to Buy (Secure Tenants only)[1]

Secure tenants of three years standing have the right to buy, and to a mortgage.

Rights and Responsibilities of the Landlord

Repairs

(*a*) Landlord to keep the structure and exterior of the dwelling in good repair.

(*b*) Landlord to keep in good repair and working order installations for supply of gas, water, electricity, drainage, heating and hot water.

(*c*) Landlord not responsible for repair of tenants' installations except where agreed in writing.

(*d*) Landlord to keep any communal areas in a reasonable state of repair and decoration.

(*e*) Tenant's rights where landlord fails to carry out repairs.[2]

Access for Landlord

(*a*) Landlord to be allowed access at all reasonable hours to inspect the condition and state of repair or carry out repairs or improvements.

---

[1] See definitions in Introduction, and p. 13, Para D *above*.

[2] *e.g.* an action in the county court for specific performance. see, Para H. *below* p. 23.

(*b*) Tenant must allow access for the above reasons where Landlord gives twenty-four hours notice in writing.

(*c*) Tenant may require confirmation of identity before granting access.

(*d*) Landlord may seek authority of magistrates' court for a warrant to enter, where necessary, due to any emergency which may result in personal injury or damage to the property.

Changes in the Terms of the Agreement

(*a*) Landlord to give written notice of any proposal to change the tenancy agreement.[1]

(*b*) Landlord to provide information on service charges on written request.

Ending the Tenancy

(*a*) Tenant to give notice to quit.[2]

(*b*) Landlord to give notice to quit, or notice of intention to seek possession, giving reasons for his action.

(*c*) Landlord to take possession, without making application to the court, where it appears after reasonable enquiries that the tenant has abandoned the dwelling.

Tenants' Associations

A recognised tenants association[3] in the privately rented sector, will usually be an organisation of the tenants of flats in one building. The association must be either recognised by the landlord, or by certificate of the rent assessment committee of the area. The association has the right to request a summary of costs relating to any or all of the flats in a block, and to inspect relevant accounts.

When the landlord consults tenants on proposed works

---

[1] Under the Tenants' Charter, secure tenants **must** be informed about decisions which may affect them, and their views must be taken into consideration.

[2] If the tenancy is for a fixed term, then the tenant may be required to compensate the landlord for any subsequent loss of rent.

[3] H.A. 1980, Schd 19, paras 20, 21.

exceeding the prescribed limit[1] he must supply at least two estimates for the work, and a copy of the notice to tenants, describing the works and inviting observations to which he must have regard.

Service charges are discussed in paragraph G of this Chapter.

The Tenants' Charter

Tenants of local councils, new towns and housing associations, *i.e.* secure tenants, are given a series of rights, known as the Tenants' Charter, introduced by the Housing Act, 1980.

The rights include:

(*a*) The right to buy your home, and your right to a mortgage.

(*b*) Security of tenure.

(*c*) The right of a near relative to succeed to the tenancy, on the tenant's death.

(*d*) The right to take in lodgers and to sublet part of your home.

(*e*) The right to improve your home.

(*f*) The right to information about your rights and obligations and those of your landlord.

(*g*) The right to be consulted about matters affecting your home or tenancy.

F. FIXTURES AND FITTINGS

Fixtures are articles attached to the property or land, and your right to remove them depends on who provided them, and the permanency of their fixing to the property. Fittings or chattels[2] may become fixtures, unless they can be

---

[1] The prescribed amount is £25 multiplied by the number of flats in the building, or £500 whichever is the greater.

[2] Moveable possessions.

removed without causing irreparable damage and were temporarily fixed for more convenient use.

In relation to tenanted property, you have a right to remove objects fixed to the house for ornament or domestic convenience, or utility, put there by you during your tenancy. As a general rule tenant's fixtures must be removed during the term of the tenancy. Once your tenancy ends, the right to remove your fixtures is severely limited, and they may become the property of the landlord.

If the fixture forms an essential feature of the house, necessary for its continued use, you would not be entitled to remove it, whoever provided it.

For example, if you install a gas fire in place of the landlord's coal burning grate, you would be entitled to remove it provided that you replaced the coal burning grate in its original state. On the other hand, if the gas fire has been provided by you, and you have been authorised by your landlord to receive grant aid, as part of a smoke control conversion, then he may insist that the appliance becomes his on termination of the tenancy.

Tenant's and landlord's fixtures may be specified in your tenancy agreement or leasing document. If fixtures are improperly removed, by either party, then a claim for damages may be entered in the civil courts.[1]

If you are a secure, protected or statutory tenant and wish to make improvements, additions or alterations to the landlord's fixtures and fittings, he cannot unreasonably refuse to give consent.[2]

G. PREMIUMS AND SERVICE CHARGES

In most cases it is illegal for you to be charged a **premium** or **key-money** when you are granted a tenancy.

[1] County court or High Court, depending on the amount claimed. See Chapter 5, paras. C and D, pp. 83 and 88.
[2] H.A. 1980, s. 81.

By definition[1] a premium includes:

(*a*) any fine or other sum, and

(*b*) any other pecuniary interest in addition to rent, and

(*c*) any sum paid by way of a deposit, other than one which does not exceed one-sixth of the annual rent, and is reasonable in relation to the potential liability in respect of which it is paid.

A **deposit**, returnable on termination of the tenancy would therefore be allowable provided that it does not exceed the scope of (*c*) above.

You are given protection by statute, as a tenant of a flat paying variable or fixed service charges.[2]

A **service charge** is defined as: an amount payable by the tenant of a flat as part of, or in addition to the rent,

(*a*) which is payable, directly or indirectly for services, repairs, maintenance or insurance, or the landlord's costs of management, and

(*b*) the whole or part of which varies or may vary according to the **relevant costs**.[3]

"flat" is defined as: a separate set of premises whether or not on the same floor, which,

(*a*) forms part of a building, **and**

(*b*) is divided horizontally from some other part of that building, **and**

(*c*) is constructed or adapted for use for the purpose of a dwelling, and is occupied wholly or mainly as a private dwelling.

Your rights in connection with service charges are: to obtain a summary of the costs on which your service charge

---

[1] R.A. 1977, s. 128(1) as substituted by H.A. 1980, s. 79.

[2] H.F.A. 1972, ss. 90, 91A as substituted by H.A. 1980, s. 136 and Schd. 19.

[3] The relevant costs are those incurred over the twelve month period prior to the tenants request, or the last accounting year's costs. If more than four flats in the block, the accounts must be independently certified.

is calculated; to inspect the landlord's accounts; to request the county court to fix the amount you have to pay for services or works, on the grounds that neither the standard of works or costs are reasonable; to request the county court to limit to what is reasonable the amount of any advance payments your lease requires you to make; if you have liability for repairs, then you have the right to be consulted before your landlord carries out major works.

In addition the statutes provide for tenants' associations[1] to be officially recognised, so that they have the right to be consulted in the same way as an individual.

These rights apply if you have bought your flat on a long lease from either a private landlord, local council, new town corporation or a housing association. The provisions also apply to tenants of private landlords and housing associations where the Rent Officer has not determined the amount you pay for service charges within the fixed fair rent.

If the landlord requests the Rent Officer to fix a fair rent, he must show separately the amounts payable for services, and give details of how he has arrived at the sums involved. You will then be consulted by the Rent Officer who will give you fourteen days to study the copies of the landlord's information, in order to prepare any points you wish him to consider.

H. REPAIR AND IMPROVEMENT

You have a right as an owner-occupier to claim the mandatory grants for improvement and repair, subject to certain conditions.[2]

As a tenant of a house or flat, it will be the nature of your tenancy agreement or lease which determines who is responsible for what. However, as previously stated[3] there

---

[1] See, para E. *above*, p. 16.
[2] See Chapter 2. Grants p. 32.
[3] See para. B above: Covenants and Agreements, p. 7.

are implied covenants between landlord and tenant, which can be relied upon in the absence of any express covenant.

The ways in which you may achieve the carrying out of repairs, which your landlord fails to execute, may be summarised as follows:

(*a*) Apply to the civil court for an order of specific performance, with a claim for damages.

(*b*) Terminate your tenancy.

(*c*) Carry out the minor repairs yourself in default of the landlord.

(*d*) Make a complaint to your local council for them to exercise their statutory powers.

Specific Performance and Damages[1]

After having notified your landlord of the repairs required, and the terms of your tenancy agreement placing him under that obligation, you must allow him a reasonable opportunity to do the work.

If there is no response, you may approach the county court, pay the required fee and submit particulars of claim, alleging a breach of the tenancy agreement and applying for an order of specific performance. The Court may, however, award you damages in lieu of an order for specific performance. The amount would reflect the difference in rental value between the house as it is, and what it would have been if the repairs had been carried out, multiplied by the number of weeks since the notice was served by you on the landlord.

A summons is served on the landlord, and if he fails to respond or wishes to contest the claim then the matter will be discussed in court. If your claim is successful, the court may order the landlord to carry out specific repairs and pay

---

[1] The HA 1974, s. 125, provides for the County Court to order specific performance of a "repairing covenant". "Repairing covenant" means: a covenant to repair, maintain, renew, construct or replace any property.

you the amount of damages, within a reasonable period. If the repairs remain unrectified then the landlord is liable to be punished for contempt of court.

Termination of Tenancy

This will be of limited value in most cases. If, however, you have signed a contract for a fixed term but can move elsewhere, then the procedure has some merit if substantial repairs are required. Legal action is unnecessary, and you can serve notice to quit on your landlord, setting out the grounds for terminating your tenancy. If he subsequently attempts to sue for lost rent up to the end of the fixed term, then you have the defence that you have rightfully terminated your tenancy.

Repair by Tenant in Default

You have a right to carry out relatively inexpensive items of repair in default of the landlord, and to recover the costs incurred from the rent. You would be unwise to embark on any form of rent strike as the landlord may well successfully sue for possession.

There are a number of important points to consider before embarking on this course of action. It must be firmly established that the landlord has the duty to repair the particular item, in accordance with the express or statutory terms of your agreement. You must give your landlord notice in writing of the need for specific repairs, and a reasonable time in which to execute them. He should be informed later by second notice that since he has not fulfilled his obligations, you intend to carry out the work and deduct the cost from future rent.[1]

The work should be done after a reasonable time, by a reputable contractor, and a written invoice and receipt obtained. You may then use the money you would have paid by way of rent to pay for the cost of repairs, after

[1] In accordance with the precedents set in *Lee-Parker v. Izzet* [1971] 3 All E.R. 1099 and *Asco Developments Ltd v. Lowes* (1978) L.A.G. Bulletin 293.

notifying the landlord of the precise amount to be set against rent.

Since it is established in law that the landlord's duty to repair is quite independant of your duty to pay rent, you run the risk of losing your security of tenure if you withhold rent as a sanction against your landlord.

Complaint to Local Council

You have the right to make a complaint to your local council, usually the environmental health department, who, if satisfied that the necessary conditions exist, may recommend the council to serve notice on the landlord requiring him to carry out the repairs within a specified period.

Some procedures require the tenant to initiate the action by making a written representation[1] where the house, though not unfit for human habitation, is in such a state of disrepair, as to interfere materially with the personal comfort of the occupying tenant.[2]

The action is discretionary upon the council, though it is unusual for them not to accede to a valid request. If the repairs are not carried out by the landlord, then the council have the power to do the work in default, and recover their expenses (reasonably incurred) from him.[3]

If the absence of repair results in the property being in such a state as to be prejudicial to health[4] or a nuisance,[5] then you have a right to make a complaint to the magistrate's court for a nuisance order[6] requiring either the landlord, or the local council to abate (put an end to) the nuisance.

---

[1] See Chapter 5, para. A, p. 79.
[2] H.A. 1957, s. 9(1)(B) as inserted by H.A. 1980, s. 149.
[3] H.A. 1957, s. 10(3).
[4] Means: injurious or likely to cause injury to health. P.H.A. 1936, s. 343(1).
[5] P.H.A. 1936, s. 92(1). See Chapter 7, para. C. p. 123.
[6] P.H.A. 1936, s. 99.

Improvement

If your house is lacking in one or more of the standard amenities[1] then you may make a representation to the local council requesting them to invoke their compulsory improvement powers.[2] These powers are again discretionary, but if satisfied that the works can be carried out at reasonable expense, the council will serve a provisional improvement notice[3] on your landlord.

The notice gives details of the improvements needed, and states the time and place of a meeting, where the matter may be discussed by all parties. In the absence of a voluntary undertaking to carry out the improvements,[4] the council may serve a final improvement notice on the owner, normally giving twelve months for the works to be done, if full standard improvements are required.

Your landlord has the right of appeal to the county court in order to have the notice quashed; he may serve a purchase notice on the council;[5] he may comply with the notice; he may do nothing and allow the council to do the work in default and recover the cost from him.

I. SUPPORT OF STRUCTURE

As the owner of a terraced or semi-detached house, you have a right of support from adjoining houses.

If a neighbour carries out structural alterations which impair the stability of your property, then he would be liable to pay compensation for the damage. He could also be prosecuted for carrying out works falling within the scope of the Building Regulations[6] without obtaining approval. The local council may, in addition, require him to put right any defects arising from his actions.

---

[1] The standard amenities are: a fixed bath or shower; a wash-hand basin; a sink; a water closet; a hot and cold water supply to the bath, wash-hand basin and sink.

[2] H.A. 1974, s. 89.

[3] H.A. 1974, s. 85(2).

[4] H.A. 1974, s. 87.

[5] H.A. 1974, s. 101, see para C above. Compulsory purchase, p. 9.

[6] Building Regulations, 1976. (S.I. 1976 No. 1676)

If an adjoining house is demolished either by its owner, or by the local council under a clearance order,[1] then the exposed wall would be made good to preserve the integrity of your dwelling.[2]

As the owner of a detached property you are entitled to lateral support from your neighbours' land. You can claim damages[3] if your land subsides as a result of your neighbours' excavations.

Where a statutory undertaker[4] carries out street works involving excavations, he is responsible for the shoring up of any adjacent building which might be affected.[5]

J. DISPLACED OCCUPIERS

It is an offence for you to use or threaten violence for the purposes of securing entry into a house for your occupation.[6]

Even if the house is yours or you would otherwise be entitled to possession as an occupier or tenant, it would still constitute an offence to use such force.[7]

However, it would be a defence in any proceedings brought against you, if you were acting as a displaced residential occupier.[8]

In the event of adverse occupation of your home, for example by a squatter, you should serve on the trespasser a notice stating your interest in the property (as tenant, owner etc.) requesting him to leave. Should he fail to do so, he will be guilty of an offence, and you would be entitled to seek the help of the courts to recover possession. The police have the power to arrest squatters.

---

[1] H.A. 1957, Part 3, as amended.
[2] P.H.A. 1961, s. 29.
[3] In the county court. See Chapter 5, para C, p. 83.
[4] Statutory undertakers include: local councils; gas regions; electricity boards; water and highway authorities.
[5] H.W.A. 1980, s. 174(1)(c).
[6] C.L.A. 1977, s. 6(1).
[7] C.L.A. 1977, s. 6(2).
[8] C.L.A. 1977, s. 6(3).

A **displaced residential occupier**[1] is a person who was occupying any premises as a residence immediately before being excluded from occupation by anyone entering those premises, or any access to them as a trespasser.

A **protected intending occupier** must satisfy all the following conditions:

You must have purchased the freehold or leasehold; require the premises for your own occupation as a residence; be excluded by a trespasser; be in possession of a written statement or certificate specifying your interest in the premises, and that you require the premises for your own occupation. The statement must be witnessed by a justice of the peace or a commissioner for oaths.[2]

The definition of a protected intending occupier is extended to include tenants of local councils and housing associations.[3]

The displaced occupier may approach the county court or high court, for an order for the recovery of possession of any premises, and it is an offence for any person to obstruct officers of the court[4] in executing such an order.[5]

K. HOMELESS PERSONS

If you are homeless or threatened with homelessness, you have a priority right to accommodation by the local council, provided that certain conditions are met;[6]

(*a*) that you have dependent children who would normally reside with you, **or**

(*b*) that you are homeless, or threatened with homelessness resulting from flood, fire or other disaster, **or**

(*c*) that you or any member of your household is vulner-

---

[1] C.L.A. 1977, s. 12(3).
[2] C.L.A. 1977, s. 7(2), (3).
[3] C.L.A. 1977, s. 7(4), (5).
[4] C.L.A. 1977, s. 10 includes sheriffs and bailiffs.
[5] See also Chapter 4, para. F, p. 75. Trespass.
[6] H.(H.P.)A. 1977, s. 2(1).

able as a result of old age, mental illness, physical disability or other special reason.

A **homeless person** is defined as a person without accommodation which he would be entitled to occupy, as well as one who cannot secure entry to his home, or who, by occupying his home would be subjected to, or threatened with violence.

You may also be homeless, if your home consists of a moveable structure, vehicle or vessel, and there is no place for you to park or moor it and reside in it.[1]

There is special provision for pregnant women and those persons who might reasonably be expected to reside with them to be given priority accommodation.[2]

A person is **threatened with homelessness**, if it is likely that he will become homeless within twenty-eight days.[3]

It is an offence to knowingly or recklessly make a statement or withhold information in order to establish the priority need for accommodation.[4] It is therefore incumbent on the local council to explain "in ordinary language" the duty of the applicant to notify the council of any change in circumstances which affects his need for accommodation, and that failure to do so constitutes such an offence.

After applying to the council for accommodation under these provisions, you should receive notification (assuming you have a postal address!) of their decision on whether or not you are regarded as being homeless, and whether you have a priority need for accommodation.[5]

If you become intentionally homeless, then you are not entitled to be given accommodation unless you fall into a priority needs category, in which case you are entitled to accommodation until you have had a reasonable opportunity to re-locate yourself. A person is **intentionally homeless**

---

[1] H.(H.P.)A. 1977, s. 1.
[2] H.(H.P.)A. 1977, s. 2(2).
[3] H.(H.P.)A. 1977, s. 1(3).
[4] H.(H.P.)A. 1977, s. 11(1).
[5] H.(H.P.)A. 1977, s. 8.

if he deliberately does, or fails to do anything, with the intent that he is likely to be forced to leave accommodation available to him, and of which he would be entitled to continued occupation.[1]

For example, if you are obliged to leave premises because you have failed to pay the rent, which on enquiry you could have afforded to pay, you would be intentionally homeless. On the other hand, if your homelessness results from genuine hardship, it would not be intentional.

[1] H.(H.P.)A. 1977, s. 17(1), (2).

CHAPTER 2

GRANTS

A. INTERMEDIATE, IMPROVEMENT, SPECIAL AND REPAIR GRANTS

These forms of grant aid are collectively referred to as renovation grants, for which local councils are in the main given discretionary powers.[1] The exceptions are the Intermediate grant which is mandatory, and the repairs grant in certain cases.[2]

Intermediate grants are intended to provide your house with any or all of the standard amenities.[3] They are available as of right, provided that the basic requirements are fulfilled. You must prove title (ownership) of the property, or seek the written consent of your landlord to carry out the scheme. The initial plans for your house must have been approved before 3rd October, 1961,[4] and there are no rateable value limitations, as for other forms of grant.

You have a right to this grant even if you do not wish to install amenities to the full standard, and obtain a further grant to put in the remainder at a later date.

In addition there is an option to claim a repairs element, which cannot exceed in value the amount eligible for impro-

[1] H.A. 1974.

[2] Where you have been required by the council to carry out repairs, under H.A. 1957, s. 9.

[3] See footnote 1, Chapter 1, para. H, page 27.

[4] H.A. 1974, s. 56(3) and D.O.E. Circular 160/74.

vements, and it is based on expense limits for either full or minor repair. If you claim the full repairs element, the council will require you to put the whole house or flat into reasonable repair. If you claim the smaller amount for minor repair, then the house will not have to meet any prescribed standard of repair.

Improvement grants are discretionary upon local councils, and are intended for improvement, repair and conversion where a more comprehensive scheme is envisaged. The items which may be included will vary slightly between local councils, but in general terms you may apply in respect of major structural improvements and repairs, including, enlargement of kitchens, renewal of ground floors; provision of the standard amenities in conjunction with the construction of a new bathroom or kitchen; provision of a septic tank where no mains drainage is available; upgrading of electrical power circuits.

Other items of improvement which may be allowed include part central heating; improvements to natural lighting; provision of a separate water service.

Other repair items may include replacement of suspended floors, stairs, windows, doors, roofs, ceilings, walls, electrical wiring and paving. As with the Intermediate grant, the value of repairs cannot exceed that of improvements.

The age and rateable value of your house will have a bearing on whether or not you qualify for an improvement grant. The limits will vary between local councils, but will not apply if the house is included in any General Improvement Area or Housing Action Area, or if you are applying as a disabled person. These factors will also influence the percentage of grant payable up to the maximum eligible expense limits, which are modified from time to time by central government.

Repair grants are discretionary[1] and the main qualifying conditions are that the repairs should be substantial and

---

[1] But see footnote 2, page 32 under which circumstances you can claim the grant as of right.

structural.[1] Routine maintenance or replacement of fixtures would not qualify for grant aid.

A repairs grant is usually available if you do not wish to carry out improvements at the same time, and is only available for houses built before 1919. However, if you wish to replace a lead water service pipe, with a pipe not made of lead, then for this purpose only, any house erected before 3rd October, 1961 would be eligible for a repairs grant.[2]

The amount of grant you would receive is a percentage of the actual approved cost, subject to the maximum eligible expense limits. There are, in addition to age, rateable value limitations, which do not however apply if your house is in a Housing Action Area, or you are applying as a disabled person.

Special grants are available only to owners of houses in multiple occupation,[3] for the provision of additional standard amenities or means of escape in case of fire. A repairs element is allowed up to the equivalent value of improvements.

Special grants are normally discretionary, but the council must give you a grant if you have been required to provide additional amenities[4] or means of escape.[5] There are no age limits for special grants.

Disabled persons are entitled to both intermediate and improvement grants, to adapt their houses where they are unsuitable or inadequate. Adaptations may be carried out for improved welfare, accommodation or employment. Provision of extra standard amenities would qualify, as would the widening of doorways, provision of ramps, chair lifts and central heating where a constant temperature is required.

---

[1] Substantial overall, and structural in that major works to walls, floors, foundations or roof are required.

[2] D.O.E. Circular 22/82, and Grants by Local Authorities (Repairs) Order, 1982 (S.I. 1982 No. 1205).

[3] See definition in Introduction p. xx.

[4] H.A. 1961, s. 15.

[5] H.A. 1980, Schd. 24.

Local councils are empowered to give improvement grants to disabled persons for the provision of alarm systems. A telephone may be provided by the local social services department, for a sick or disabled person who may be at risk owing to the absence of such facility.[1]

Elderly and severely disabled persons on low incomes are also entitled to higher grants for thermal insulation.[2]

Disabled persons are not subject to the property age and rateable value limits, which apply to other applicants for some types of grant.

General Conditions

For all categories of grant aid there are certain common factors, influencing your eligibility and the amount of grant you are likely to receive.

Eligible expense limits are determined by central government, and from time to time are modified, together with the age and rateable value criteria. This is done in order to provide for constantly changing housing needs and priorities, and inflation. Grants are paid by local councils out of their Housing Investment Programme, and owing to the cash limits imposed by an annual allocation they may terminate consideration of new applications for those grants which are discretionary, when the available funds are committed in any one year.

For these reasons you are advised to ask the council for your area, to give you the current eligible expense limits and percentage grants applicable to your house, for the types of grant aid required. Local councils have discretion to give you an increased percentage grant, where they consider that you are unable to pay for your share of the work without undue hardship, and you may also be entitled to borrow the balance from the council on agreed terms.

As a general rule, and subject to the eligible expense

---

[1] C.S.D.P.A. 1970, s. 2(1) not in the form of a grant.
[2] See para. D, page 43.

limits, the percentages of the approved costs you might receive would be as follows:

Priority cases: houses in need of substantial and structural repair, lacking any of the standard amenities, unfit or in a Housing Action Area—75%
Houses in General Improvement Areas—65%
All other cases—50%

In cases of hardship, the council may give you a grant of up to 90% of the eligible expense in priority cases, or up to 65% in all other cases.

The **general conditions** which must be fulfilled in order to qualify for a renovation grant are as follows:

(*a*) You must not start any work until all grant, Building Regulations and Planning approvals have been given.

(*b*) Subject to the exceptions previously stated, the plans for your house must have been passed before 3rd October, 1961.

(*c*) You must possess either the freehold, or a leasehold interest with a minimum of five years to run.

(*d*) You must declare your intention of future occupation, or of letting for at least five years (seven in a Housing Action Area) following completion of the works.

(*e*) You must complete the works within twelve months although the council may grant an extension of time for a valid reason.

(*f*) You must improve your loft insulation[1] in accordance with the current standard.[2]

(*g*) To qualify for an Improvement grant, your house must have an anticipated life, after renovation, of 30 years.

---

[1] See para. D, page 43.
[2] H.I.A. 1978.

(*h*) If you do any of the work yourself, you cannot claim for the cost of your own labour.

Repayment of Grant

You would not usually have to pay any grant back as an owner-occupier, if you sell your house to another owner-occupier, or make it available for letting. Grants are not intended, however, to improve second or holiday homes.

As a landlord, you are required to give a certificate of letting as in (*d*) above, and there may be further conditions as to the type of letting, otherwise the whole grant or part of it may have to be repaid with interest.

If you are a tenant who has received a grant with your landlords' consent, you cannot be required to repay it.

Contracts

The council would have no binding interest in any contract between you and your builder, and any dispute is a matter to be resolved by you. The council would not be responsible for the standard of work of the builder you employ, although they would satisfy themselves that the work done warranted payment of the grant.

Applications for Grants

Most local councils make informal surveys on request, in order to advise applicants and avoid abortive applications. The council's surveyor will advise you what is grant aidable, and what additional works, if any, they will require. He will subsequently provide you with the necessary application forms, and inform you of detailed drawings and estimates, together with any other approvals which may be required.

Agency Services

Recognising that making applications for grants requires so much form filling, and that applicants may be discouraged by this, some local councils have set up agency services. These usually include making all necessary applications for the grant, Building Regulations approval and Planning

Permission, obtaining estimates and drawings, and possibly discussing financial arrangements with your bank or building society. The fee for the service is grant aidable, as would be any Architect's fee under normal circumstances.

B. SMOKE CONTROL GRANTS

If you live in an area declared to be included in a Smoke Control Order,[1] then you have a right to a grant towards the cost of adapting coal-burning grates[2] to appliances which will burn smokeless fuels.[3]

The grants are mandatory, and the council will have satisfied themselves by sample or full survey of the houses concerned, that the necessary funds exist to finance conversions. They will also have made sure that sufficient supplies of smokeless fuels are locally available.

After having made the Order, and before submitting it to the Secretary of State (DOE) for confirmation, the council must publish their intentions, giving details of the streets affected and the manner in which objections should be made.[4] The public notices appear in one or more newspapers circulating in the area, and are posted, usually to street lighting columns, around the district concerned.

If you wish to object to the confirmation of the Order, then you must do so in writing within the period allowed, to the local council. The council are obliged to take any objections into account, giving objectors the opportunity of being heard. If the Order is confirmed, the works of conversion take place during the period before the Order officially comes into operation. If the area comprises mainly new properties then this may be a short period of two or three months, though six to twelve months would be the normal time where a significant number of adaptations are required.

---

[1] C.A.A. 1956, s. 11(1).
[2] *i.e.* "open fires" capable of burning only coal.
[3] C.A.A. 1956, s. 12(1).
[4] C.A.A. 1956, Schd. 1 as substituted by L.G.(PL)A. 1980, Schd. 2.

Applications

The council will supply you with the application form, which should be completed and returned to them together with an estimate of the costs, and written authorisation from your landlord, if you are a tenant and claiming the grant yourself.

As an owner-occupier, the choice of appliance and fuel is yours, provided that they are "approved appliances"[1] and "authorised fuels".[2]

As a landlord you can either carry out the adaptations yourself and claim the grant, or, if your tenant prefers an alternative installation give him permission in writing to do the work and claim the grant.

If you commence any work before your application is approved, then you may forfeit your right to the grant. As with other forms of grant aid, there are maximum cost limits, specified by central government which are from time to time modified. You should enquire what the current cost limits are before making application, as you will have to bear all costs above the seventy percent grant, which you are entitled to receive. The council have discretionary powers to make grants of up to ninety percent of the approved cost in cases of hardship.

The works must be carried out before the operative date of the order, and on completion you should send a claim form to the council, together with a written invoice from the contractor. The council may send an officer to inspect any existing appliance, to ensure that conversions are necessary, and they may visit again on completion, to see that the works claimed for have been done. Any contractual arrangement between you and your heating installer would not be binding on the council.

---

[1] Taken from the approved lists published by the Solid Smokeless Fuels Federation; Solid Fuel Advisory Service; Gas Council; Electrical Development Association.

[2] Include: Sunbrite, Anthracite, Phurnacite, Coalite, Rexco, Homefire, Housewarm and washed singles and trebles of coal for use only on specific appliances, electricity, and gas, amongst others.

Grants are not available for houses or flats built after 16th August, 1964.[1]

C. NOISE INSULATION GRANTS

Road Traffic

Where a highway authority[2] creates a new road, or carries out improvements to existing roads, you have a right to claim a grant towards the cost of noise insulation, where you are affected by additional noise above the specified level.[3]

The object is to enable residents to benefit from noise reduction in their homes, by installing double glazing, supplementary ventilation, venetian blinds and double or insulated doors.

Insulation grants may also be offered under these provisions in respect of construction site noise.

All dwellings are eligible, provided that they were occupied before the new or improved road was open to traffic. If your house is subject to a Compulsory Purchase Order or is within a Clearance Area, it will be ineligible. Otherwise, all living rooms and bedrooms which have one or more windows or doors exposed to noise at or above the specified level, qualify for treatment, as would the rooms of any existing extension or conversion so situated.

Eligible dwellings or parts of dwellings are shown on a map or list produced by the highway authority, which is available for public inspection within six months of the road opening or completion of the improvement.

Applications are not essential, as the authority will make you an offer of insulation on some or all rooms listed, which

---

[1] H.A. 1964, s. 95(1).

[2] Includes: County Councils; the Greater London Council and London Borough Councils.

[3] Noise Insulation Regulations, 1975, (S.I. 1975:1763) "specified level" means: a noise level of L10 (18-hour) of 68 dB(A). L10 is the noise level in dB(A) which is exceeded for 10% of the time. L10(18-hour) is the arithmetic average of all hourly L10 values during the period 0600–2400 hrs, on a normal working day.

is open for acceptance by an owner-occupier for a period of 12 months after the road has opened. As a tenant you have the exclusive right of acceptance within three months of the offer being made, but thereafter the landlord has a shared or exclusive right of acceptance.

The amount of grant is intended to cover the actual cost, and since the council (highway authority) will be carrying out much of the work by sub-contract, they will have negotiated discounts with contractors and suppliers. It is unlikely, though not impossible, that you could have the work done for a lower figure. You have a right to employ your own contractor, though it is imperative that you obtain details of the **reasonable cost limit** from the council, as any excess of the limit will have to be borne by you.

The installation must comply with the Regulations,[1] and be completed within twelve months of accepting the offer. On completion, you should send an application for payment to the council, together with a written invoice. If you intend doing the work yourself, you cannot claim for the cost of your own labour.

A word of **caution** is appropriate here, in that you may block your means of escape in case of fire, by installing fixed panel double glazing. People have been trapped in their homes, as a result of being unable to get out of the windows. It is always possible for a do-it-yourself enthusiast, armed with a length of aluminium track, a sheet of glass and a screwdriver to install a hazardous fixed panel system.

Aircraft Noise Insulation

Airports under the control of the British Airports Authority[2] may be required by the Secretary of State, Department of Trade, to make grants available towards the insulation of buildings.[3]

---

[1] Noise Insulation Regulations 1975, Schd. 1.

[2] Heathrow, Gatwick, Stanstead, Prestwick, Edinburgh, Aberdeen and Glasgow.

[3] Noise Insulation Grants Schemes, *e.g.* in the case of Heathrow the scheme is prescribed by Statutory Instrument 1980 No. 153, as varied by Statutory Instrument 1981 No. 652.

Those airports controlled and owned by local councils[1] are empowered to give grants by local Acts of Parliament.

Grant schemes are usually of finite duration, and apply only to existing dwellings. New properties, built in the areas so affected are normally required by the local council to have satisfactory sound insulation.

The schemes are designed to cover the cost of double glazing, special ventilation systems, roof insulation, sealing of chimneys and necessary incidental repairs.

Applications

If your house falls within the area defined by the scheme, you have a right to claim grant aid either as an owner or tenant (with the landlords' written consent) provided that the property is eligible. The schemes are mainly administered by local councils, either on behalf of the British Airports Authority, or as airport owners themselves.

You should apply using the form provided by the council, giving your name, full address, specification of the works and an estimate of the costs. The works will be required to meet the standards laid down in the scheme, and will be subject to maximum cost limits on which a percentage grant is paid.

If an application is refused, the council may be required by the scheme, to give a written statement of the reasons at the applicant's request.

The rate of grant varies according to the noise level contours, rather like Ordnance Survey altitude contours, but relating to measured sound emission. The properties most seriously affected may attract grant aid of 90%–100% of the approved cost: those further away from the airport (generally) and affected to a lesser degree, 60%–75%, depending on the particular scheme.

As with all other forms of grant, you should not do any work, until you have received approval from the council,

---

[1] Luton, East Midlands, Leeds–Bradford, Manchester, Birmingham, etc.

who will tell you how much grant you are likely to receive. On completion, you should submit a claim form, signed and dated, together with the contractor's invoice. The council will inspect the works, to verify that they comply with the requirements of the scheme. Following a satisfactory inspection, payment will be authorised.

D. LOFT INSULATION

You have a right to claim a grant towards the insulation of your loft, water tanks and pipes in roof spaces and hot water cylinder, provided that you have no existing insulation.[1]

The Homes Insulation Scheme also provides for the cost of cutting an access into the loft, where none exists, but is generally not applicable to flat roofs, or other areas of roof where there is no space other than the depth of the joists or rafters.

Applications

You should complete the council's application form and send it to them.[2] They may wish to inspect the property to satisfy themselves that no insulation already exists, and in any event you should not commence the work until written approval has been given.

You should only use materials specified in the scheme, and see that they are laid to the required thickness. You may employ a contractor to do the work, but it is wise to ensure that he is used to this kind of work, and that he is aware of the council's specifications. You are entitled to claim for the contractor's installation charges, as well as for the materials used.

The council will insist that the works are completed within a specified period, and you must claim the grant within that time, by producing an invoice for labour and/or materials

[1] Homes Insulation Scheme 1982, made under H.I.A. 1978 s. 1(1).

[2] If you are making application as a tenant, your landlords written consent is required.

together with a signed claim form. They may again inspect the property to ensure that the works have been done in accordance with the requirements of the scheme, following which, payment of the grant will be authorised.

There are maximum cost limits, and the grant received will be a percentage of the approved cost which may vary from 66% to 90%. The higher rate of grant is payable to the elderly and severely disabled who are on low incomes.

CHAPTER 3

PUBLIC SERVICES

A. DRAINAGE

The law on drainage examined in detail, would fill this volume many times over. It is only feasible therefore to illustrate the more commonly encountered provisions, as far as your rights and responsibilities are concerned. Your rights may arise in common law, that is, by precedents set in the courts over the years, or in statute law by Acts of Parliament.

Definitions

Your rights will depend greatly on the extent to which your house is served by drains, private sewers or public sewers. It is therefore necessary to give several definitions:

"**drain**" means a drain for the drainage of one building or of any buildings or yards appurtenant to buildings within the same curtilage.[1]

"**sewer**" does not include a drain . . . but . . . includes all sewers and drains used for the drainage of buildings and yards appurtenant to buildings.[2]

---

[1] P.H.A. 1936 s. 343(1) . . . a pipe in exclusive use by one owner or occupier.

[2] P.H.A. 1936 s. 343(1) . . . a pipe in **shared** use by more than one owner or occupier.

"**public sewer**"—is a sewer which is vested[1] in the water authority[2] and for which the water authority is responsible for cleansing and maintenance.[3]

Most, but not all sewers constructed by the local council or water authority at their expense are public sewers.

"**private sewer**"—means a sewer which is not a public sewer, as defined above.[4]

There are cases where you could be called upon to pay the cost of maintenance of a length of public sewer, although the statutory provisions on this point are extremely complex.[5]

If, for example, you are the owner of a property which is served jointly with other properties by a common drain, and all such properties were built prior to 1st October, 1937,[6] then the common portion of the drainage system **may be** a public sewer,[7] even though not formally adopted[8] (see below). The water authority or its agent would be responsible for the cleansing and maintenance of this sewer, but may at its discretion recharge the relevant owners for works of maintenance.

Adoption

Sewers which are adopted become public sewers, for which the water authority is responsible, and once adopted they remain so for evermore.

It is an advantage to the property developer to construct his sewers to meet the requirements set by the water authority for adoption. It may be easier and cheaper, to construct sewers to the standard required to meet the Buil-

---

[1] means: rights, interests, estate etc. possession of which is determinately fixed in the authority and is not subject to any contingency.

[2] P.H.A. 1936, s. 20 as substituted by W.A. 1973, s. 40 and Schd. 8.

[3] P.H.A. 1936, s. 23, as amended by W.A. 1973, s. 14.

[4] P.H.A. 1936, s. 343(1).

[5] P.H.A. 1936, s. 24.

[6] P.H.A. 1936, operative date.

[7] Sometimes referred to as a "section 24 sewer" or a "former combined drain".

[8] Adoption in relation to sewers, is the transfer of responsibility by agreement for cleansing and maintenance.

ding Regulations (which is likely to be lower than that set by the water authority) but, prospective purchasers are reassured by an agreement[1] between the developer and the water authority to adopt.

Once the developer has sold you a house, he has no remaining responsibility in drainage law, to deal with defects or blockages which may occur in private sewers.[2] It is by no means certain that your new house on a modern estate, will be served by a public sewer, and you may have a continuing maintenance commitment.

The status (whether public or private) of the sewer serving your house should have been revealed on the enquiries of the council's records,[3] made by your solicitor when purchasing the property. If the enquiries reveal that a notice has been served by the local council[4] requiring maintenance to be carried out on a length of private sewer,[5] then you could negotiate a retention on the sale, or an indemnity from the vendor, to cover your share of the estimated costs.

You may experience some difficulty in persuading the local council, acting as agents (usually) for the water authority, to adopt an existing private sewer. The criteria for adoption can be summarised as follows:

(*a*) The sewer must be constructed to the adoptable standard, or improved to that standard.

(*b*) The sewer by its adoption, must be of benefit to the general sewerage system.

If you are aggrieved by the refusal of a local council, acting as the water authority's agent, to adopt your private sewer, you have a right of appeal to the Minister of Health. You may appeal any time after notice of refusal of your

---

[1] P.H.A. 1936, s. 18.
[2] He may still be liable under an N.H.B.C. guarantee, or for negligence.
[3] Enquiries of District Councils. Form Con 29A (outside London)
[4] Under P.H.A. 1936, s. 39; L.G.(M.P.)A., 1976, s. 35; P.H.A. 1961, s. 17, as amended by L.G.(M.P.)A. 1982. See also Chapter 7, para. C., p. 123.
[5] Or drain, water closet, cesspool etc.

application has been given, or if no such notice is received, within two months of your application.[1]

Duties of the Water Authority

It is the duty of every water authority to provide public sewers for effectually draining their area, and to provide sewage disposal works for treatment of the contents.[2]

The authority or its agents are obliged to keep and maintain public sewer maps, which are available for inspection free of charge, usually at the local council offices.[3]

Right to connect

You also have a right as an owner or occupier to connect your drain or private sewer to a public sewer, at your own expense, provided that where both foul and surface water sewers are available you do not connect to the wrong pipes.[4] You must give notice of your intention to the local council, who have the right to undertake the work themselves, if they wish. You are entitled to break open the street for laying or maintaining the drain, provided that you give the council notice of your intention.

Repair

You may request the council, in writing to undertake the cleansing or repair of drains, water closets, sinks or gullies. Application may be made either by the owner or occupier, who will be responsible for re-imbursing the council their reasonable expenses.[5]

If you have been served with a notice, by the local council, which requires the removal of blockages and/or the repair of drains or private sewers, you have rights of appeal. An appeal may be brought against service of the notice, and

---

[1] P.H.A. 1936, s. 17(3).
[2] W.A. 1973, s. 14(1).
[3] P.H.A. 1936, s. 32(1) as amended by W.A. 1973, s. 40 and Schd. 8.
[4] P.H.A. 1936, s. 34.
[5] P.H.A. 1961, s. 22.

you can defend any proceedings brought by the council to recover its costs from you.[1]

Surface Water Drainage

Your statutory rights are basically the same as for foul water drainage, in respect of the right to make connections, etc.

If you are building a new house, or creating an extension and there is no available surface water drainage, the council may require you[2] to construct a soakaway, to deal with surface water and roof water.

There are common law rights of drainage which can be relied upon, in the absence of a statutory provision. You must accept any surface water from your neighbour's land, which flows to you as a result of natural contours. Similarly, you have a right to discharge such water to the owner whose land is lower than yours.

If your neighbour carries out modifications to his property, or land which results in a significantly increased flow of surface water, which floods your property, he may be liable for creating both a common law and a statutory nuisance. This situation might arise by the blockage of a drain, or construction of a paved area where physical damage to your land, buildings or vegetation results. In the case of a common law nuisance, you are entitled to claim damages and/or seek an injunction directing your neighbour to cease committing the nuisance. In the event of the matter being taken up by the local council, as a statutory nuisance, they may use their powers to seek the provision of proper drainage.[3]

Where a blocked dyke or stream floods your property and it is not part of the public sewer system,[4] then the owners on both sides of the stream at its point of blockage, have a

---

[1] See Chapter 7, para. C. p. 123.

[2] Under the Building Regulations 1976. (S.I. 1976, No. 1676)

[3] P.H.A. 1936, s. 39(1).

[4] Unless it takes discharges from septic tanks or surface water from roads, and was constructed before 1.10.37, or is otherwise adopted as a public sewer.

duty to remove the obstruction if caused by them, or, if caused by a third party and they have failed to abate the nuisance when they knew or might reasonably have known of its existence. If they are not liable,[1] you may request the local drainage board[2] or the local council to clear out the stream, but they are not obliged to do so.

If the blockage results in conditions prejudicial to health or a nuisance, the local council may serve notice[3] requiring the person(s) responsible for the blockage to remove it.

B. ELECTRICITY

Supply

You have a right to a regular and efficient supply of electricity, and to be protected from any personal injury, fire or other danger arising from its supply or use.[4] This is conditional upon your entitlement to receive a supply, not having been disconnected for non-payment of bills, or due to an unavoidable breakdown beyond the control of the Electricity Board.

If you have no supply laid on to your house, you may, together with any five owners or occupiers along your street, requisition a supply of electricity, by serving notice to that effect on the Board.[5]

The Board may counter-serve a notice of refusal within fourteen days after receipt of such requisition, unless the persons requesting the service agree to guarantee to take a sufficient quantity of electricity for three years, at the rate specified by the Board, which will produce annually such reasonable sum as the Board may determine.[6] The Electricity Board may also appeal to the Department of Trade and

---

[1] See Chapter 7, para. B: Private Nuisance p. 119 and the case of *Sedleigh-Denfield v. O'Callaghan*.

[2] L.D.A. 1976, s. 18.

[3] P.H.A. 1936, ss. 259, 93.

[4] Electricity Supply Regulations 1937, as re-enacted by E.A. 1947, s. 60(1) and amanded by E.A. 1957, Schd. 4.

[5] E.L.(C)A. 1899, para. 24(1), (2) of the Schedule.

[6] E.L.(C)A. 1899, para 25(1) of the Schedule.

Industry that the requisition is unreasonable, otherwise, the requisition is binding if notice of refusal is not given or an appeal lodged within fourteen days.

You may request the Board to provide a supply to your premises, if they are situated within fifty yards of a distributing main.[1] You may be required to finance the cost of laying supply lines on your property, and the cost of laying such lines beyond a distance of sixty feet from the Board's distributing main.

The Board are responsible for the electric lines, either overhead or underground, up to and including the consumer unit (meter). Your responsibility is for all wiring and appliances from that point onwards. Your rights extend to the provision of a meter which is certified as accurate, and the Electricity Board commits offences by installing or failing to remove uncertified meters,[2] although certain alterations[3] and uncertified meters[4] are permitted.

The Board will provide you with an application form for supply. They will also carry out a survey and provide a quotation for the cost of providing a supply.

Testing of Meters

You can require the Electricity Board by notice in writing, to have the meter tested.[5] If the inaccuracy is found to be more than 2½% plus, or 3½% minus, the Board will pay for the expenses of testing, and re-adjust the charges accordingly. If the meter is found to be within those limits, the expenses of testing may be charged to you.

Re-sale of Electricity

If you are a tenant, your landlord may charge you for electricity which he buys from the Board, and subsequently sells to you through a secondary meter. This he may do by

---

[1] E.L.(C)A. 1899, para. 27 of the Schedule.
[2] E.A. 1957, s. 30.
[3] Meters (Permitted Alterations) Order, 1958, (S.I. 1958 No. 1061.)
[4] E.A. 1957, s. 30(5).
[5] E.L.(C)A. 1899, para 57 of the Schedule.

either charging an inclusive rent, or installing credit or coin operated prepayment meters. The landlord is legally permitted to sell you electricity at a higher price to meet his expenses, subject to maximum rates set by individual Boards.

Charging above the maximum is not a criminal offence and the only course of action open to you, is to sue for recovery of the excess in the civil courts. The Electricity Board is not responsible for the accuracy or setting of private secondary meters, through which electricity is resold.

The maximum you can be charged is specified in x pence per unit, and y pence per day, and applies to the resale of electricity for domestic purposes, which includes dwellings, hotel rooms, holiday accommodation and premises in multi-occupation.[1]

The area Electricity Board Consultative Councils are usually prepared to consider and advise on any case brought to them.

Other problems arise such as disconnection, where you have paid the landlord, but the landlord fails to settle his account with the Board. In addition to pursuing a case in the civil courts, you may make a representation to the local council, to arrange for the "restoration and continuation of electricity supplies".[2] In practise, the local council would be unlikely to exercise this discretionary power, if the outstanding debt resulting in disconnection is very large, since the Board would require some significant discharge of the debt before restoring the supply. It would be an added disincentive for them, if recovery proceedings against the landlord were unlikely to be viable, owing to his financial position, but the council does have a right to recover its expenditure by requiring the tenant to pay his rent to them direct.

---

[1] A house occupied by persons who do not form a single household. H.A. 1969, s. 58.

[2] L.G.(MP)A. 1976, s. 33.

Disconnection

The electricity and gas industries have agreed a Code of Practice[1] for the protection of domestic consumers, who cannot pay their bills and are threatened with disconnection.

Consultative Councils

If you have a complaint about goods or services supplied to you by the Electricity Board, you should first contact their local office, in an attempt to resolve the matter. If this does not produce a satisfactory result, then you are entitled to approach a member of the local Consultative Council committee, whose names and addresses are displayed in the showrooms and offices of the Board.

Consultative Councils were established by the former Minister of Power[2] and are representative of consumer interests.

Safety

Requirements for the safety of equipment designed or suitable for use in your house, are administered by the Consumer Protection Departments of County or London Borough Councils, on behalf of the Department of Prices and Consumer Protection.[3]

The Institution of Electrical Engineers have produced "regulations"[4] designed to ensure safety especially from fire and shock in the use of electricity. The compliance of your installation with these regulations is deemed to satisfy certain[5] of the Regulations of the Secretary of State for Energy, and the Secretary of State for Scotland.

These Regulations are designed for your safety, and for ensuring a proper and sufficient supply of electricity.[6] They

---

[1] "*Paying Gas and Electricity Bills*" (Revised July 1982) obtainable from Citizens Advice Bureaux, Gas Consumers Council, Electricity Consultative Councils, and Consumer Advice Centres.

[2] E.A. 1947, s. 7.

[3] Electrical Equipment (Safety) Regulations, 1975 (S.I. 1975 No. 1366).

[4] Fifteenth Edition 1981. Not a Statutory Instrument.

[5] Electricity Supply Regulations, 1937, regulations 26, 27, 28, 29, and 31.

[6] Electricity Supply Regulations, made under E.(S)Acts, 1882 to 1936.

require Electricity Boards to declare the type of current, number of phases (AC), the constant frequency and voltage.[1] The supply must be maintained for the use of customers entitled to it, except for the purposes of testing when you are entitled to twenty four hours notice of interruption. In the case of an emergency, the supply may be interrupted for any necessary period, without such notice.[2]

Any difference which may arise between you and the Electricity Board, with regard to your installation, can be determined, in England and Wales, by an inspector appointed by the Secretary of State for Energy.[3] You may make application to the Secretary of State yourself or through an agent. The Electricity Board may also be an applicant.

Repairs

Most Electricity Boards will undertake installations, improvements and repairs for you on agreed terms.

If you live in a tenanted property and your electrical wiring is defective or dangerous, then you should notify your landlord forthwith, in order to have the installation checked by a competent electrician and repaired as necessary.

If the landlord fails to act upon your notification then you may approach your local council with a request for them to exercise their powers. If the wiring is seriously defective, then the property may be regarded as unfit for human habitation in that condition.[4] If the tenancy was created before 1961, then the person responsible for repair would depend on the terms of the tenancy agreement.[5]

---

[1] Electricity Supply Regulations, 1937, Reg. 34. Single phase alternating current at a nominal 240 volts (± 6%) and at a nominal frequency of 50 Hertz (± 1%).

[2] Electricity Supply Regulations, 1937, Reg. 35.

[3] Electricity Supply Regulations, 1937, Reg. 33.

[4] H.A. 1957, s. 9.

[5] H.A. 1961, s. 32, which states that there is an implied covenant for the landlord to keep in repair and working order, installations for the supply, amongst other things of electricity, in respect of tenancies created after the passing of the Act.

C. GAS

Supply

You have a right to a continued supply of gas, if you are an owner or occupier entitled to a supply, and it has not been terminated owing to non-payment of bills, or contravention of safety regulations.[1]

The Gas Corporation may be prosecuted and fined unless the supply failure was due to one of the above reasons or that it was due to circumstances beyond their control.[2] e.g. a fractured main.

You are entitled to inspect the quarterly statement of gas testing for calorific value[3] and pressure[4] which must be displayed at Gas Region showrooms and offices.[5]

Whose pipes?

Before considering your rights any further, it is important to distinguish which parts of the gas supply pipes, fittings and meters belong to whom.

The Gas Corporation and its Regions own and are responsible for, the maintenance of all mains and **service pipes** up to and including the **primary meter**, the index reading of which constitutes the basis of the charge for gas used on the premises. Your responsibility is for the **installation pipes** and all controls and appliances for the use of gas on the premises.

Escapes

The Gas Corporation are duty bound to prevent escapes of gas, within twenty-four hours, if you give notice in writing of the escape.[6] The Corporation may be prosecuted and fined for failing to execute the repair of any main or service

---

[1] Gas Safety Regulations, 1972, (S.I. 1972 No. 1178).

[2] G.A. 1972, Schd. 4, para. 6, as amended by G.A. 1980.

[3] i.e. the heat produced by a unit volume of gas which should (for natural gas) be not less than 38.5 Megajoules/cubic metre.

[4] Should be not less than 12.5 mbar.

[5] G.A. 1972; Gas (Testing) Regulations, 1949, (S.I. 1949 No. 789).

[6] G.A. 1972, Schd. 4 para. 23, as amended by G.A. 1980.

pipe, unless they can prove that it was not reasonably practicable for them to do so within that period, and provided they prove that the escape was effectually prevented, as soon as it was reasonably practicable.

Entry and Repair

You are entitled to twenty-four hours notice in writing of the Corporation's intention to enter your house for the purposes of removing any pipes, meters, fittings or apparatus.[1]

If your property has been entered by force, in order to make good an escape or for the purposes of removing meters etc., the Corporation are responsible for leaving the premises as secure as they were on entry. Any damage must be made good, or compensation paid.[2]

Re-sale of Gas

As a tenant, your supply of gas will usually continue as long as the bills are paid. A landlord who buys his gas from British Gas and sells it to you, must not charge more than the maximum resale price fixed by them.[3]

Your landlord may recover the cost of gas supplied to you either by levying an inclusive rent, or by the installation of secondary credit or coin operated prepayment meters.

There is a possibility that you could lose your supply if the landlord subsequently fails to pay his bills. If the landlord's reading of your meter is demonstrably incorrect, or you have paid for gas not supplied by way of advance rent, then you may sue in the county court to recover your loss.

There may also be an implied covenant, under which the landlord is obliged to keep in repair and working order, installations for the supply of gas.[4] The local council may,

[1] G.A. 1972, Schd. 4 para. 25(1) as amended by G.A. 1980, and the Gas Safety (Rights of Entry) Regulations, 1983, (S.I. 1983 No. 1575).
[2] G.A. 1972, Schd. 4, para. 26.
[3] G.A. 1972, Schd. 4, para. 12.
[4] H.A. 1961, s. 32 only if the tenancy was created after the passing of the Act.

on receipt of a written representation, arrange for the restoration or continuation of supplies of gas.[1]

Testing of Meters

The Gas Region is responsible for the accuracy of the primary meter, and if you consider that the amount of gas shown to have been consumed is inaccurate, you can request them to check it. If the meter is defective the Gas Region will pay for the testing of the meter and come to an agreement with you on reimbursement.

If the meter is found to be correct, then you may be required to pay for the cost of testing.

Consumer Councils

If you have a complaint about the performance of an appliance or the quality of service provided by the Gas Region, which is not rectified by them, you are entitled to request your regional Gas Consumers Council to investigate the matter. The names and addresses of the Council's local members are posted in Gas Region offices and showrooms.

D. TELEPHONES

As a British Telecom customer, you are entitled to take complaints about equipment, or about special directory entries which are chargeable, either to arbitration or to an independent complaints panel, depending on the nature of your complaint.[2] Members of the arbitration or complaints panel are drawn from members of the Chartered Institute of Arbitrators.

In order to assist its customers, British Telecom have produced a booklet[3] explaining what to do when things go wrong, and advising on how best to deal with disputes.

---

[1] L.G.(MP)A. 1976, s. 33.

[2] British Telecommunications Act, 1981.

[3] "*Code of Practice for Telecommunication Services*" obtainable from local telephone area offices and Citizens Advice Bureaux.

E. WATER

Supply

It is the duty of the water authority to supply water within their area.[1] Duties are also placed upon local councils to make checks on the sufficiency and wholesomeness of water, and to notify the water authority of any shortcomings in these matters.[2]

You have the right to demand and receive from the water authority, a supply of water sufficient for domestic purposes.[3] This means a supply sufficient for drinking, washing, cooking and sanitary purposes, but not for any bath having a capacity in excess of fifty gallons.[4]

The right of supply extends to provision of water for a profession, where the premises are mainly a dwelling, and, where water is drawn from a tap inside the house, a supply for watering a garden, washing vehicles, and for horses for private use. The right does not extend to provision of water for laundries or food preparation, except where such food is to be consumed on the premises.

The rights are conditional upon your property being within the limits of supply, and that a proper service pipe is provided, as well as the settling of any water rate. The water authority would not be obliged to supply water if any of the fittings[5] are not in accordance with the byelaws.[6]

Failure

The water authority are liable to a fine and daily penalty for failing to maintain a supply, in respect of which a water rate has been paid or tendered, and may in addition have

---

[1] W.A. 1973, s. 11(1).
[2] W.A. 1973, s. 11(2).
[3] W.A. 1945, Schd. 3 Part 8, para. 30.
[4] Measured to the centre line of the overflow pipe.
[5] Water fittings include: pipes (other than mains) taps, cocks, valves, ferrules, meters, cisterns, baths, water closets, soilpans and other similar apparatus used in connection with the supply and use of water. W.A. 1945, Schd. 3 para. 1.
[6] Made under W.A. 1945, s. 17.

a civil liability.[1] There is, however, no liability placed on the water authority, where the failure is due to:

(*a*) frost, drought, unavoidable accident or necessary works, **or**

(*b*) failure of the householder to comply with the Water Acts or byelaws.

Whose pipes?

As with the other public utilities and services there are portions of the service pipes which belong to each party. A "**service pipe**" is that length of pipe from a main, to any premises up to the stop tap, usually beneath the kitchen sink in a house. The service pipe is divided into two portions; the "**communication pipe**" for which the water authority have responsibility; and the "**supply pipe**" for which the house owner is responsible. The communication pipe is that length from the main up to and including the stop cock, usually found on your property boundary (in the pavement), and the supply pipe is the remainder up to your house.

Escapes of water

Where an escape of water occurs, however caused, from a communication pipe or main of the water authority, which causes loss or damage, the authority is liable[2] for such loss or damage, unless it is self inflicted by an owner, occupier or his agent.[3]

There are defences available to the water authority, in that they are not generally liable for loss or damage suffered by excepted statutory undertakers.[4]

New Supplies

If you propose to erect a building for which a supply of water is needed, you can require the water authority to lay

---

[1] W.A. 1945, Schd. 3, para. 30(2).
[2] W.A. 1981, s. 6(1).
[3] W.A. 1981, s. 6(2).
[4] W.A. 1981, s. 6(7)(c) for definition.

the necessary mains to such point that you can connect your buildings at a reasonable cost.[1]

To qualify under these provisions, your house must be within the limits of supply, geographically, of the water authority.

You may be required by the authority, to deposit one eighth of the cost of providing such mains, every year for twelve years, or until the total water rates payable annually on that service equals or exceeds that sum.[2] The water authority are obliged, however, to deduct from the cost any amounts received by them in respect of water supplied in that year from those mains.

You may also be required to deposit the total expense of such installation, out of which the annual charge is deducted.

If you cannot agree with the water authority on the points to which mains are to be laid, you have a right of appeal to the Secretary of State.[3]

If the authority fail, without reasonable excuse, to comply with the request within three months (either of receipt or following the Secretary of State's decision on appeal) then they are guilty of an offence.[4]

Repair

You may request the water authority to supply, install repair or alter, any water fitting allowed by the byelaws whether supplied by them or not, on such terms or charges as are agreeable.[5]

If you are the occupier of a house without a supply of wholesome water sufficient for domestic purposes, the local council may serve notice on the owner, requiring him, if reasonable, to connect the house to an available water main,

---

[1] W.A. 1945, s. 37(1) as amended.
[2] W.A. 1945, s. 37(1)(a)(b), (2).
[3] W.A. 1945, s. 37(3) as substituted by H.A. 1949, s. 46.
[4] W.A. 1945, s. 37(4) as substituted.
[5] W.A. 1945, s. 35(1).

or provide a supply within a reasonable distance.[1] There is a right of appeal, by the owner within twenty-eight days after service of the notice, to a magistrates' court.[2]

Your landlord may be required to repair a water closet, if it is in such a state as to be prejudicial to health or a nuisance, for example, by having a defective water supply.[3]

Consumer Interests

Every water authority is obliged to make a report on arrangements for representation of consumer interests, subject to guidelines issued by the Secretary of State.[4]

The authority has a duty to put into effect and maintain these arrangements, as approved by the Secretary of State.

The effect of this will be to establish consumer councils on similar lines to those which exist for the gas and electricity industries. Consumer interests are defined as including the interests of recreational users which would include angling clubs, and those organisations involved in water sports, using rivers and reservoirs under the control of the authority.

---

1 P.H.A. 1936, s. 138 as amended by W.A. 1945, s. 30, and by W.A. 1981, s. 5.
2 See Chapter 5, para. B, p. 81.
3 P.H.A. 1936, s. 45(1).
4 W.A. 1973, s. 24A as inserted by W.A. 1983, s. 7.

CHAPTER 4

PEACEFUL OCCUPATION

A. POLLUTION

Domestic Air Pollution

If you live in a Smoke Control Area[1] it is an offence to emit smoke from your domestic chimney, by burning an unauthorised fuel.[2,3] The local council may take legal action against offenders in the magistrate's court, where, on conviction, you could be fined.[4]

You are obliged, in such an area, to burn one of the authorised smokeless fuels, or particular grades of coal only on approved appliances.[5] It is also an offence, punishable by fine, to sell bituminous coal in a smoke control area, unless specially packed and marked for use on particular approved appliances.[6]

Where you are troubled by a neighbour's garden bonfire, and your reasonable intercessions have failed to improve matters, you can request your local council to take up the matter. If they are satisfied that a nuisance exists, they will

[1] See Chapter 2, para. B, p. 38.
[2] Definition of "authorised fuel" see footnote 2, page 39.
[3] C.A.A. 1956, s. 11(2).
[4] C.A.A. 1956, s. 27(1).
[5] See footnote 1, page 39.
[6] C.A.A. 1968, s. 9.

serve notice requiring the nuisance to be stopped. (abated) If the person responsible fails to desist, the council may apply to the magistrate's court for a nuisance order. The court may, after having heard both parties, issue the nuisance order requiring compliance. They may also impose a fine and a daily penalty, for each day during which the nuisance continues.[1] The local council ultimately have power to abate nuisances themselves and recover their costs from the person(s) who fails to comply with the nuisance order.

Similar action can be taken by the local council in dealing with offensive odours.

Industrial Air Pollution

Your local council have responsibility for the control of emissions of smoke, grit, dust and fumes from commercial and industrial premises. It is an offence for dark smoke[2] to be emitted from a factory chimney, unless temporarily unavoidable through breakdown, lighting up or suitable fuel being unavailable. If you are seriously inconvenienced by such emissions you should contact your local council's Environmental Health Department.

Some of the major industrial processes, such as chemical and cement works, power stations and steel works are under the control of H.M. Industrial Air Pollution Inspectorate. The Inspectors operate as part of the Health and Safety Executive, and the addresses of your local District Inspector can be found in telephone directories.

The Industrial Air Pollution Inspector ensures that emissions to atmosphere from these works are minimised or rendered harmless in accordance with the requirement for industries to adopt the "best practicable[3] means"[4].

---

[1] P.H.A. 1936, s. 94.

[2] "Dark smoke" means smoke which if compared in the appropriate manner with a Ringelmann Chart, would appear to be as dark or darker than Shade 2.

[3] "Practicable" means reasonably practicable having regard to local conditions and circumstances, and to the current state of technical knowledge and financial implications.

[4] "Means" include the design, installation, maintenance and manner and periods of operation of plant and machinery, and the design, construction and maintenance of buildings and acoustic structures.

It is an offence to burn insulation with the intent of recovering metal from cable, unless it is done at a place registered by the H.M. Industrial Air Pollution Inspectorate.[1]

Domestic Noise

If you are the occupier of a dwelling and have reason to be aggrieved owing to noise made by a neighbour within his premises, you have a right to take formal action in an attempt to resolve the problem.[2]

The kind of disturbance which this procedure can cover includes barking dogs, noise from radio, television, hi-fi, shouting, banging doors, D.I.Y. activities at unreasonable hours, etc.

It should be remembered that semi-detached houses terraced properties and flats are seldom sound proof. You will then from time to time be able to hear activities of this nature. If however such noise is so frequent and prolonged as to interfere with your normal activities as an occupier, then an informal approach to your neighbour should be the first step.

If this fails to have the desired effect, you should put your complaint in writing, requesting your neighbour to reduce the disturbance. You should allow a reasonable time for your neighbour to comply, keeping copies of all correspondence.

If all attempts at persuasion fail, then you are entitled to make a complaint on your own behalf to a magistrate's court. It is not essential to employ a solicitor, as the justices clerk or a magistrate will, if satisfied that there is a case to answer, witness the form of complaint which you will have completed.

The defendants will be summoned to appear to answer

---

[1] C.P.A. 1974, s. 78, as amended.

[2] C.P.A. 1974, s. 59, as amended, which covers action taken by an individual. The noise may also be actionable by the local council under s. 58, as a nuisance. See Chapter 7, para. C, p. 123.

your complaint, which should include details of dates and times of the nuisance, its duration and description and information on how it affects your occupancy. If the court finds in your favour, then they will make an order directing that the nuisance is abated and preventing its recurrence. If you lose the case, then you may be liable to pay the costs of the other side.

Industrial Noise

As with air pollution, your local council are responsible for controlling noise emission from commercial and industrial premises.[1] If the noise amounts to a nuisance then the council will serve notice on the person responsible for the nuisance, or the owner or occupier of the premises if he cannot be found.[2] An appeal may be made against the notice, to a magistrates court within twenty-one days.

Subject to appeal, failure to comply with the notice is an offence, which on conviction is punishable by fine. For the above purposes noise includes vibration.[3]

Where the local council wish to control noise from an industrial or manufacturing area for the benefit of surrounding houses, they may make a Noise Abatement Order.[4] The order has the effect of preventing a deterioration of the noise "climate" by registering existing levels of noise emission from each of the factory premises, which cannot in future be exceeded without the council's consent.

Noise in Streets

Your travelling butcher, baker, fishmonger or ice-cream salesman, is permitted to operate a 'loudspeaker' between the hours of noon and seven p.m.[5] It must be used solely for the purposes of informing members of the public that the commodity is on sale from the vehicle.

---

[1] And noise from any other premises, if it amounts to a nuisance.
[2] C.P.A. 1974, s. 58.
[3] C.P.A. 1974, s. 73(1).
[4] C.P.A. 1974, s. 63 and Schd. 1, as amended by L.G.(PL)A. 1980.
[5] C.P.A. 1974, s. 62(3).

If the "chimes" are operated outside this period, or in such a way as to give reasonable cause for annoyance to persons in the vicinity, an offence is committed.

The Department of the Environment has issued a Code of Practice[1] giving guidance on methods of minimising annoyance or disturbance caused by the operation of such chimes.

A similar code of practice exists for the guidance of model aircraft enthusiasts.[2]

Both these Codes of Practice may be taken into account by the local council and the magistrate's court, in deciding whether or not an offender has adopted the "best practicable means" of minimising emissions.[3]

Under the council's byelaws for "good rule and government", certain other offences may exist, for causing noise in streets.[4]

B. LIGHT AND PRIVACY

Light

You have no automatic right to daylight received over your neighbour's land, or to an unspoilt view from your house, unless you have entered into an agreement that neither will obstruct the other's light.

A neighbour can erect a building or extension which cuts off your light, unless you are protected by:

(*a*) the Building Regulations[5] which require a zone of open space to windows in new structures, or

(*b*) planning restrictions,[6] or

---

[1] Code of Practice on Noise from Ice-Cream Van Chimes Etc., 1982, D.O.E. made under s. 71, C.P.A. 1974.

[2] *Code of Practice on Noise from Model Aircraft*, D.O.E. 1982.

[3] C.P.A. 1974, s. 72.

[4] See para. E below, p. 73.

[5] Building Regulations 1976, S.I. 1976 No. 1676), Reg. K3.

[6] T.C.P.A., 1971.

(*c*) guarantees to sufficient light to make your house comfortable to live in "by reasonable standards"

Guarantees in (*c*) above may be obtained in several ways:

(*a*) your title deeds may specify your right to such light, or

(*b*) you may have a common law or statutory[1] right to light acquired by continuous use for twenty years or more, or

(*c*) you may have previously entered into an agreement with your neighbour, in the form of a mutually restrictive covenant.

As far as the Building Regulations are concerned the dimensions of the zone of open space, can only be established from the proposed windows and their position in the facade of the building. General interpretation indicates that such a zone should exist within the boundary of the proposed or extended property.

If you become aware of an application for planning permission for a building or extension which will obstruct your view, you are entitled to object to the local council. If, as a result of nearby development your view is spoilt, you may be able to claim a rate reduction.[2]

At common law, a right of light is presumed to exist if it appears that there has been a user of it, as of right, since the beginning of legal memory.[3] Since your house is likely to have been built since the twelfth century, your claim to a right of light may be more confidently established in the principle of a "lost modern grant".

If you can show that you have enjoyed light without interruption for a minimum period of twenty years, then the courts may presume the grant of an easement which has

---

[1] Prescription Act, 1832, s. 3.

[2] In the form of a "proposal for alteration of the valuation list" see Chapter 5, para I, p. 101.

[3] A.D. 1189.

since been lost. You do not have a natural right to light, as such a right can only be acquired as an easement.

The amount of light to which you become entitled to after use of it for twenty years, is so much of it as is required for ordinary purposes. In other words you cannot object to any obstruction of it, unless it amounts to a nuisance.

Interruption of Light

You may register a notice with the local council, to be entered in the Land Charges Register,[1] which acts as a notional obstruction to your neighbour's light.[2] The notice must specify the existing buildings and the size and location of the notional obstruction to which the notice is intended to be equivalent. The notice takes effect as if the light had been obstructed, and remains in force for one year.

During this time, your neighbour may sue in the courts for a declaration as if his light had actually been obstructed, claiming his easement under an "ancient" or "lost modern grant", and requesting cancellation or variation of your registration. If he fails to claim within that period, then he loses his remedy, and you may continue to obstruct his light, subject to any planning or building regulations approvals on the construction of buildings.

Privacy

In general there is no statutory or common law right to privacy. A neighbour can insert new windows, subject to the constraints already mentioned in this Chapter, even though they give a view into your house.

Someone with a camera and telephoto lens could take photographs of you in your home, without committing an offence, provided that the photographs are not defamatory.

---

[1] Provided that the Lands Tribunal have certified that notice has been given to the persons affected, or that urgency dictates the registration of a temporary notice.

[2] R.L.A., 1959.

C. TREES

Lopping

You have a right to cut off the branches of your neighbour's trees where they cross the boundary between your respective properties. The branches, however, do not belong to you, and must be handed back to your neighbour, together with any fruit on them. Such lopping must be done from your side of the fence, unless as is always preferable, you can arrive at some amicable agreement for pruning.

Where the growth of trees in an adjacent property interferes with an easement, for example a right of way or of light, then you can sue for interference with such a right without having to prove actual damage.

Roots

If the roots of a tree in your garden spread under your neighbour's ground, damaging his buildings, you will be liable to pay him compensation for the damage caused. It is no defence to say that the tree was there before your neighbour's house was built, or that it was not planted but self sown.[1] On the other hand, if your neighbour's house was built in such a position that any reasonable person would appreciate the risk, then the courts may decide that your neighbour is not entitled to claim damages.

Any tree roots that trespass, can be severed by the owner of the land onto which they are trespassing. However, if damage is caused by drainage of water from your land by poplar roots, you cannot recover damages if the roots are all within your neighbour's land.[2]

If your tree roots have trespassed into your neighbour's land, it is no defence to plead ignorance of the situation, and that natural growth was the cause of damage.

---

[1] *Davey v. Harrow Corporation* [1957] 2 All E.R. 305, C.A.
[2] *Butler v. Standard Telephones* [1940] 1 K.B. 399.

Overhanging Trees

You may be liable for damage caused by your tree overhanging a highway, if you have actual or constructive knowledge that it is a hazard to traffic.[1] It would be a defence to prove that the result was not for want of action by you, but was the act of a trespasser, or a secret and unobservable operation of nature, such as subsidence, when neither owner or occupier can be liable.[2]

Preservation Orders

You may be prevented from cutting down, topping or lopping a tree which is subject to a Tree Preservation Order made by the local council.[3] Such an order makes it an offence to carry out such work unless you obtain consent from the council.

When an order is made, all owners and occupiers of the land on which the tree(s) stand are notified, and the opportunity is given for objections to be made, within twenty-eight days of the date of notification. You should, if so inclined, object in writing, and if the council consider it necessary, a public inquiry will be held.

In an emergency the council can make an order which has immediate effect, which is a provisional order for six months or until confirmed, whichever is the earlier.

Orders which are confirmed are kept at the council's offices, and are entered in the Register of Local Land Charges. You remain responsible for the tree(s) even though an order has been made, and you must apply for consent before carrying out any work on them. If consent is refused, you are entitled to appeal to the Secretary of State within twenty-eight days of such refusal.

You do not require consent, where an order is in force for:

(*a*) cutting down a tree under a forestry dedication

---

1 *British Road Services v. Slater*, [1964] 1 All E.R. 816.
2 *Wringe v. Cohen* [1939] 4 All E.R. 241 C.A.
3 T.C.P.A. 1971, ss. 59–62, 102, 103, 174, 175, as amended.

covenant, an approved plan of operations, or where a felling licence has been issued to you as a resident of a conservation area.

(*b*) cutting down, topping and lopping a tree which is:

(*i*) dead, dying or dangerous,

(*ii*) necessary for abatement or prevention of a nuisance, which is actionable in law.

(*iii*) in accordance with a statutory obligation,

(*iv*) by or at the request of a Government Department or statutory undertaker,

(*v*) where immediately required for carrying out approved planning permission,

(*vi*) a cultivated fruit tree in an orchard or garden.

D. RIGHTS OF WAY

A right of way may be in the form of an easement which can either be granted or acquired by prescription.[1]

You can grant a right of way by agreement with an adjacent owner or owners, in consideration of an agreed sum.[2] The rules governing acquisition of a right of way by prescription are similar to those governing light.[3]

You can prevent a person acquiring a prescriptive right of way over your land, by ensuring that the way is periodically obstructed.

Shared Drives

The title deeds of your house will show the limits of any shared path or drive. It may be that you and your neighbour each own one half of the drive, with a right of way over the other half. Alternatively, one of you may own the entire access, whilst the other has a right of way over it.

---

[1] P.A. 1832, or at common law.

[2] See Chapter 1, para. B: Covenants and agreements, p. 7.

[3] See para. B above, p. 66.

If you are a sole owner of a shared drive, path or other access, you have no right to obstruct it.

Public Rights Of Way

Local councils are required to keep definitive maps and statements indicating public rights of way, which are available for inspection, free of charge, at all reasonable hours at their offices.[1] They are also required to keep such documents under continuous review.[2]

The map and statement must show every road used as a public path, by one of three descriptions:[3]

(*a*) *A byeway open to all traffic*

A highway over which the public have a right of way for vehicular and all other kinds of traffic, but which is used by the public mainly for the purpose for which footpaths and bridleways are so used.

(*b*) *A bridleway*

A highway over which the public have rights of way on foot, or horseback or leading a horse, with or without a right to drive animals along it.

(*c*) *A footpath*

A highway over which the public have a right of way on foot only, and does not include a highway at the side of a public road.[4]

E. AMENITY

Delapidated Buildings

If the local council are satisfied that a building or structure in their area, is in such a ruinous or delapidated condition that it is seriously detrimental to the amenities of the neighbourhood, they may serve notice on the owner. He will be required to do one of two things:

---

[1] W.C.A. 1981, s. 57(5).
[2] W.C.A. 1981, s. 53.
[3] W.C.A. 1981, s. 54(2).
[4] W.C.A. 1981, s. 66(1).

(*a*) repair and restore the building or

(*b*) demolish it, and remove surplus materials from the site.[1]

The owner has rights of appeal against the notice[2] to a magistrate's court, within twenty-one days of the date of service of the notice. The local council have the power to carry out the work in default of the owner and recover their expenses 'reasonably incurred'.

Untidy Land

The remedy available to the council in this case, is serving notice requiring the removal of accumulations if resulting in disamenity[3] or infestations of rats or mice.[4]

Protection of Amenity

The council are obliged by law, to consider the beauty of the landscape or other amenities of the locality, when preparing proposals for the provision of houses. They must also consider the desirability of preserving existing buildings or works of architectural, historic or artistic interest.[5]

The council are authorised to spend up to the amount raised by a 2p rate, on certain matters not otherwise authorised by statute.[6] This might cover environmental improvements in the interests of all or some of the inhabitants of their area. This provision also enables the council to contribute to say, a local conservation society, but it is entirely discretionary upon them.

Byelaws for Good Rule and Government

Your local council is empowered to make byelaws for the good rule and government of their area;[7] for the suppression

---

[1] P.H.A. 1961, s. 27(1). The owner has the choice.
[2] See Chapter 5, para. B, p. 81.
[3] T.C.P.A. 1971, s. 65, see Chapter 9, para. D, p. 146.
[4] P.D.P.A. 1949, s. 4.
[5] H.A. 1957, s. 149(1).
[6] L.G.A. 1972, s. 137.
[7] L.G.A. 1972, s. 235(1).

of nuisances and for regulating the use of public open spaces.

All byelaws must be confirmed by the appropriate Secretary of State, and you are entitled to inspect them free of charge, at all reasonable hours at the council's offices.

Byelaws for good rule and government cover an almost limitless number of offences, all designed for the protection of the amenity of your neighbourhood. The Secretary of State has made model byelaws, which include clauses for controlling: music near houses, churches and hospitals; noisy hawking; touting; wireless loudspeakers, gramophones and organs; shooting galleries; indecent language; violent behaviour on school premises; fighting; indecent bathing; indecent shows; nuisances contrary to public decency; wilful jostling; loitering at church doors; advertising vehicles; flags; defacing pavements; advertising bills; broken glass; carrying soot; carrying carcases; dangerous games near streets; spitting; bulls; cycling on footpaths; fouling of footpaths by dogs and noisy animals.

Byelaws in respect of public open spaces, regulate the user's conduct, and may be made by local councils or other bodies who manage such areas. (e.g. National Trust)

Litter

If any person throws down, drops or deposits and leaves anything in any public place (in the open air) which is likely to cause defacement by litter, he will be guilty of an offence.[1]

If you witness such an act, you are entitled to bring proceedings on your own behalf in a magistrate's court, in the same way as any local council. Any person found guilty of such an offence would be liable to a fine on summary conviction. The courts in sentencing any person would have regard to the nature of the litter, and the likelihood of injury to persons, animals and property.[2]

---

[1] Litter Act, 1983, s. 1.
[2] Litter Act, 1983, s. 1(4).

F. TRESPASS TO LAND

Definition

Trespass to land is committed by one who **intentionally** or **negligently** enters the land (including buildings) of another person in possession of that land, or, by a person who having entered with permission, does some act in excess of the permission, or remains on the land after it has expired.

Trespass may be a criminal act resulting in prosecution, or a civil wrong (a tort) for which the remedies are damages and/or injunctive relief.

Criminal trespass

You may be prosecuted, fined and/or imprisoned for trespassing on foreign diplomatic missions or consular premises,[1] or trespassing in any enclosed or ornamental garden set apart in any public place.[2]

You may also be fined for trespassing on railway lines, sidings, embankments etc.,[3] or entering or remaining on any military camp, or interfering with the execution of manoeuvres.[4]

Civil trespass

As far as the integrity of your land is concerned, the invasions which result in trespass have been established in case law (precedent).

The most common form of trespass, is unauthorised personal entry onto another person's land. However, trespass not only applies to the unauthorised entry of persons, bu may be committed by a person throwing an article onto your property; leaning a ladder against your wall; allowing a creeper to grow on it,[5] or piling rubbish against it.[6]

---

1 C.L.A. 1977, s. 9.
2 T.G.P.A. 1863, s. 5, as amended.
3 B.T.C.A. 1949, s. 55, as amended.
4 M.A. 1958, s. 8, as amended.
5 *Simpson v. Weber* (1925) 41 T.L.R. 302.
6 *Westripp v. Baldock* (1939) 1 All E.R. 279.

Objects such as footballs or golfballs which land on your garden may give rise to an action for trespass, if proved to have been struck with that intention or where such invasion arises from negligent play. Here we enter a legal no man's land. The objects do not become yours, and you are not entitled to touch them, pick them up or use them. The owner cannot retrieve them without your consent, otherwise he or she will commit trespass. If you are so minded, you are entitled to let them lie where they fall to rot. If the entry of such objects has caused some damage, you are entitled to seize the article, keeping it safe until you receive an offer of amends.

There are several conditions which must be satisfied before trespass can be said to have taken place. You must show that you were in possession of the land; that the interference was direct and that it was intentional or negligent.

Possession

It is necessary to prove that you were in actual possession of the land (e.g. as owner or tenant) at the time of the trespass. It is not necessary for you to prove title or any other legal interest in the land, as this would discriminate against many people who have enjoyed lengthy peaceful occupation, in bringing proceedings for trespass.

Trespass by squatters (unlawful dispossession) is dealt with in Chapter 1.[1]

Your possession of land, extends to the column of air of equal cross-sectional dimensions above it, and to the land beneath the surface. Anyone who legally extracts minerals (e.g. coal or oil) from beneath your property, or flies through the air space above it does not however commit trespass, but may still be liable for any material loss or damage caused by these actions.

With these exceptions, the slightest infringement of your land or crossing of the boundary is sufficient to give rise to

---

[1] para. J, p. 28.

trespass. It may be possible to obtain an injunction against a neighbour requiring him for example, to remove an advertisement which directly infringes your air space.[1]

Firing a bullet across your neighbours' land would in certain circumstances be trespass. In the Tasmanian cat case[2] the defendant shot a cat on the plaintiff's roof, and was held liable for damages in respect of trespass as well as for the value of the cat.

Putting a hand through a window; sitting on a fence or flying a kite across a neighbour's land would be actionable, although if no danger, damage or inconvenience could be proved, the damages awarded would probably be nominal.

Direct or indirect Invasion

The unauthorised planting of a tree on another's land would be a direct invasion and an actionable trespass. On the other hand, to allow the roots and branches of a tree to grow under and over another's land is an indirect invasion and not a trespass, although it may be an actionable nuisance.[3]

Intention and Negligence

In order for trespass to occur, entry must be intentional or negligent. A person thrown onto another person's land does not commit trespass, but the thrower does.[4]

If you entered someone else's land with the honest but mistaken belief that you owned it, or had a right to be on it, you would still commit trespass[5] as the entry would be intentional.

You have no right to enter your neighbour's land in order to repair your own property[6]—that would also constitute trespass, as the entry would be direct and intentional.

---

[1] *Kelsen v. Imperial Tobacco Co. Ltd.* (1957) 2 Q.B. 334.

[2] *Davies v. Bennison* (1927) 22 Tas.L.R. 52.

[3] *Lemmon v. Webb* (1894) 3 Ch. 1. See also Chapter 7, para B, p. 119 for private nuisance.

[4] *Smith v. Stone* (1647) Style 65, Eng. Rep. Vol. 82, p. 533.

[5] *Basely v. Clarkson* (1682) 3 Lev. 37, Eng. Rep. Vol. 83.

[6] *Hewlitt v. Bickerton* (1947) C.L.C. 10504.

Lawful Entry

Many people will have permission to enter your land, such as the milkman, postman, dustman etc. Indeed as an occupier you tacitly invite and permit any member of the public coming on lawful business, to enter your garden gate and come to the front door. The exception to this is where the person knows or ought to know that his entry is forbidden, for example by a notice saying "No canvassers or hawkers".

Certain local government officials, civil servants and authorised personnel of the public utilities, have statutory rights of entry to your land, and do not commit trespass when so authorised.[1]

However, in all these cases a trespass will be committed if the entrant exceeds the scope of the permission granted. For example, if you invite a person into your house to use the staircase, you do not invite him to slide down the bannisters.[2]

Remedies

You may sue in the County or High Court[3] for damages and/or an injunction preventing a recurrence of the trespass. The amount of damages awarded would depend on the loss you have suffered as the "injured" party.

If someone tips refuse on your land, you would be entitled to damages for depreciation of its value.[4]

---

[1] See Chapter 6, para A, p. 107.
[2] Scrutton L.J. in The Calgarth (1927).
[3] See Chapter 5, paras C and D, p. 83.
[4] *Whitwham v. Westminster Brymbo Coal & Coke Co.* (1896) 2 Ch. 538.

CHAPTER 5

APPEALS

A. LOCAL COUNCIL

You may make representations to the local council on various matters, occasionally as an essential prerequisite for enabling them to exercise their statutory powers.

You may for example be a tenant, whose house is in a poor state of repair, or lacking in one or more of the standard amenities.[1] You are entitled to make a written representation if your house, though not unfit for human habitation, is so defective as to interfere materially with your physical comfort.[2] You may also request the council to compel your landlord to install a bath, wash-hand basin, sink, water closet and a hot and cold water supply.[3]

Form of Representation

No forms are prescribed, though your representation must be in writing, and include your full name and address; the name and address of your landlord or his agent, and a

[1] For definition of standard amenities, see footnote 1, page 27.

[2] H.A. 1957, s. 9(1)(B), as inserted by H.A. 1980, s. 149.

[3] H.A. 1974, s. 89. See also Chapter 1, para. H, p. 23.

request for the council to use their powers to assist you. Your letter (it is always wise to keep a copy) should be signed, dated and addressed to the local council.

If the council fail to respond or refuse to accede to your request, you should write again, and in the latter case, ask them to give you their reasons. It should be remembered, however, that the powers referred to are discretionary, and provided that the council have duly considered your representation, and not acted unreasonably, then a refusal may mean an end to the matter.

If you feel that your representation has not been duly considered, or has been unreasonably refused, you may refer your complaint to the Ombudsman, who would investigate and determine whether or not injustice has arisen from maladministration.[1]

Appeals

The relaxation of controls by central government over local councils in certain matters, has done away with the requirement for some local public inquiries and appeals to the Secretary of State.[2]

In respect of smoke control orders[3] objections are now considered by the local council, there being no appeal to the Secretary of State. It would still be open to you to bring proceedings in the High Court, if you thought that the council had exceeded their statutory powers.

Similar provisions now exist in respect of the confirmation of and appeals against Noise Abatement Orders, declared by the local council.[4] Noise Abatement Orders apply only to commercial and industrial premises, though the benefits to the householder arise from control of the noise "climate".

To object to a smoke control order, you should write to the council within the period allowed for objections,

---

[1] See para. F, page 96.
[2] L.G.(PL)A. 1980, s. 1.
[3] C.A.A. 1956, s. 11 and Schd. 1, as substituted by L.G.(PL)A. 1980, Schd. 2.
[4] C.P.A. 1974, s. 63 and Schd. 1, as substituted by L.G.(PL)A. 1980, Schd. 2, para. 14.

following publication of their public notice in your local newspaper. An objection should relate to specific matters arising from the order in question, and not be in the form of a general complaint against such orders.

B. MAGISTRATES' COURT

Service of notices on you by the local council requiring you to do something with your house, are negations of the freedom to do what you like with your property. Parliament has therefore laid down strict rules for infringement of this freedom.

Grounds for Appeal

These will vary, according to the Statute under which the notice is served, but in general, you lose most avenues of appeal, if you do not act within the period specified for appeals on the notice. Under public health legislation, the grounds for appeal against a notice, are as follows:

(*a*) that the notice is not justified, by the section of the Act under which it is served.

(*b*) that there has been some material informality, defect or error in, or in connection with, the notice.

(*c*) that the works required are unreasonable, unnecessary, or that your proposal for alternative works has been unreasonably refused.

(*d*) that the time allowed for you to comply with the notice is not reasonably sufficient.

(*e*) that the notice should have been served on your landlord, or on you instead of the landlord.

(*f*) that some other person[1] ought to contribute towards the cost of the required works.[2]

If you appeal under (*e*) or (*f*) above, you must serve a copy of your notice of appeal on each other person referred

[1] Being the owner or occupier of premises to be benefited.
[2] P.H.A. 1936, s. 290.

to. The appeal must be made within twenty-one days of the date of service of the notice, and is made in the form of a "complaint for an order" which is regarded as the bringing of an appeal.[1]

Form of Appeal

There is no prescribed form for the purposes of the Public Health Acts and much associated legislation, but you should submit a statement in writing, which includes your full name and address, occupation, and age. You should state that you are the owner or occupier of the premises specified in the notice. You should list the requirements of the notice, and state your grounds of appeal, concluding with a request that the court summon the council to a hearing to answer your appeal.

The Hearing

When the court has listed the matter for hearing, you will be notified of the date and time when you should attend the court, together with any legal representative or witnesses you wish to assist you.

The terms of the notice will be read out to the court, and the council may call witnesses (council officials or other residents) to verify that service of the notice was justified. You or your solicitor may cross-examine the council's witnesses.

You will then be required to state the grounds of your appeal, and call your witnesses (if any) to support your case. Together with your witnesses, you may be cross-examined by the council's solicitor.

The court will decide having heard both parties, to allow or disallow your appeal. If you lose your appeal then you must comply with the notice or with the order of the court. Failure to do so, may result in the council doing the work themselves, and recovering their expenses from you.[2] You

---

[1] P.H.A. 1936, s. 300.
[2] See para. C, page 83.

may be entitled to recover or be ordered to pay the costs of the other party, depending on whether you win or lose.

Appeals to a Higher Court

If you are aggrieved by a decision of the magistrates' court, you may appeal to the Crown Court.[12] If the court upholds your appeal, and the council's decision is varied or reversed, the council have a duty to comply with any court order, by issuing any required consent, certificate or other document.

You cannot appeal to the Crown Court where either party might have referred the matter, under a statutory provision, to arbitration.[2] An arbitrator is usually appointed by agreement between the parties, or, if agreement cannot be reached, by the Secretary of State.

C. COUNTY COURT

The County Court hears civil cases only. You may wish to **bring** proceedings in the County Court *e.g.* to claim compensation (damages) for damage caused to your property by a third party, to seek the Court's assistance in preventing a recurring trespass or nuisance or in respect of a breach of a covenant. On the other hand you may wish to **defend** any proceedings brought by a third party, or to **appeal** against a Notice served under the Housing Acts.[3]

If you are acting for yourself, then as a "litigant in person" you have a right of audience in all English courts.

Claim for Damages

If you wish to claim compensation for damage caused to your property you would normally enter your case in the County Court unless your claim exceeds £5,000 in which

---

[1] The Crown Court replaced Quarter Sessions and Assize Courts, by virtue of the Courts Act, 1971. The Crown Court is presided over by a High Court Judge, Circuit Judge or Recorder, who may sit alone, or with not less than two, or more than four magistrates when hearing appeals.

[1] P.H.A. 1936, s. 301.

[3] *e.g.* H.A. 1957 ss. 9, 11, 17, 20, 27. Section 9 amended by H.A. 1980, s. 149.

case it would be heard in the High Court (unless the parties consent in writing to the matter being resolved in the County Court).

To enter a case in the County Court you are required to lodge in Court:

(*a*) A completed "**request for Summons**" Form (blanks are provided by the Court).

(*b*) Two copies of the **Particulars of Claim** plus one copy for each additional Defendant. As you would imagine "Particulars of Claim" set out the details of your claim (as the Plaintiff) against the person you are suing (Defendant). Specimen particulars of claim are obtainable from any County Court office.

(*c*) The appropriate "**Plaint Fee**" which is related to the amount of your claim.

You will be issued with a "Plaint Note" showing the fee you have paid and the number allocated to your case. You will find that the County Court staff will be happy to advise you on the procedures, but they are not authorised to provide legal advice.

Before starting any legal action of this kind, it is wise to consider the financial position of your opponent, as there is little to be gained in winning a case if the judgement debt cannot be paid.

Default Summons

If your claim is for a sum of money (*e.g.* a debt or damages for personal injuries) the action will proceed by way of default summons.

In this case no hearing date is fixed and if the Defendant has not paid the debt and costs, or filed a defence and/or counterclaim within 14 days of the Summons being served on him, you are entitled to enter judgment. To do this you simply complete a "request for entry of judgment" form and hand it into the County Court office with your Plaint

Note. You can ask for the debt and costs to be paid immediately, or within a fixed number of days, or by instalments.

If the defendant has filed a defence and/or counterclaim the Court will normally set the case down for a preliminary hearing (called a pre-trial review). If the matter cannot be resolved satisfactorily, the case will then be set down for hearing before a judge or registrar. (See "Trial" and "Arbitration" later).

If your claim is for an unliquidated sum *e.g.* damages for personal injuries, the default summons procedure described above is followed with one exception. You can still enter judgment against the Defendant in the circumstances described, but this time the judgment will be one "for damages to be assessed". This means that upon receipt of your "request for entry of judgment" form the Court will allocate a date on which you will be required to attend to prove the amount of your claim.

Fixed Date Summons

Such a Summons is issued in every case where the Default Summons procedure with its comparative simplicity cannot be used *e.g.* in actions for possession of land, recovery of goods, an order restraining a neighbour from committing a nuisance (injunction) or requiring the Defendant to comply with a Covenant or other agreement (specific performance).

No fourteen day default judgment is available and when you have entered the case in Court a day will be allocated usually for a pre-trial review, but sometimes for the trial itself, as in actions for the recovery of land.

Small Claims

Any claim which does not exceed £500 is described as a small claim. If the Defendant files a defence to a "small claim" the case is automatically referred to **arbitration**. It is open to a party to object to the arbitration reference on certain grounds *e.g.* if the case involves complex questions of law and/or fact or fraud. It is open to all parties to agree that the case be tried not at an Arbitration Hearing but in open Court.

The main feature of the automatic reference to arbitration is that the loser does not have to pay the winners costs of the hearing (which he would normally be ordered to do if the case was heard in open court). This is commonly referred to as the "no costs rule". It is important to note, however, that the arbitrator can order a party to pay such costs if they have been incurred through unreasonable conduct in relation to the proceedings.

Defending a claim for default works expenditure

Where local councils and statutory undertakers are given the powers to execute works where you default in complying with a notice, they must demonstrate that their expenses are "reasonably incurred". You are barred from defending on any ground on which you could have appealed to the Magistrate's Court.

If you consider that the work could have been done for a lower sum *e.g.* by employing fewer workmen or using cheaper and/or fewer materials you may file a defence to the claim, if you have been served with a Summons. Together with the Summons and particulars of claim, you will have received a "form of admission, defence and counterclaim". You should complete the relevant section of the form giving your grounds for defending the claim, and if you wish you may insert in the relevant section the sum which you think is reasonable for the cost of the works. You must complete the defence and return it duly signed to the County Court office, within fourteen days of the date on which you were served with the Summons.

If the claim is a "small claim" the Court will, upon receipt of your defence, refer the dispute to arbitration automatically (see "small claims" earlier). Remember that the burden of proof is on the Plaintiff (local council or statutory undertaker) to show that the expenses incurred are reasonable, not on you as Defendant to prove that they are unreasonable.

Housing Acts Appeals

Appeals may be made by an owner against a Closing Order, Demolition Order, or a notice to repair or improve a dwelling. In addition to appealing on the grounds that the notice is erroneously served, the most frequent ground of appeal is that the repair or improvement can (or cannot) be carried out at reasonable expense. In determining this, regard is given to the estimated costs of the works necessary to make the house "fit" for human habitation or provide missing amenities, and the estimated value of the house when the works are complete. The age, character and locality of the house are also considered, when arriving at this theoretical reasonable standard.

Arbitration

In addition to the "no costs rule" there are two other features of an Arbitration hearing. Firstly there is the informality. The dispute is settled in private (as opposed to open Court) and the strict rules of evidence and procedure are dispensed with. The Arbitrator's decision is described as an "award". Your rights to have the award set aside (*i.e.* to appeal) are limited. The grounds for setting aside an award are where the Arbitrator had no jurisdiction, where he was guilty of misconduct or where the award contains a material error of law on its face. An application to set aside an Arbitrator's award is heard by the judge.

You do not qualify for legal aid (irrespective of your means) for a claim involving less than £500 unless the reference to arbitration is rescinded.

Trial

If your dispute remains unresolved and if it is one which cannot be made the subject of an Arbitration hearing, it will go to trial either before the County Court Registrar or before the Judge.

The Registrar has power to deal with claims up to £500; larger claims and appeals from decisions of the Registrar/ Arbitrator are heard by the Judge. The case is concluded in open Court and the strict rules of evidence and procedure are followed. You may choose to conduct your own case, whether as Plaintiff or Defendant although legal representation is the rule rather than the exception in open Court hearings.

Judgment

At the conclusion of the case, the judge, registrar or arbitrator will give his decision. Subject to the rules governing costs at Arbitration hearings, the loser will usually be ordered to pay all the winner's costs. The loser may be ordered to pay the judgment debt immediately, by a certain date, or by instalments.

D. HIGH COURT

The High Court comprises three divisions, Chancery Division, Queen's Bench Division and Family Division. All three divisions have equal jurisdiction, although for administrative purposes, particular types of cases are allocated to particular divisions.

The Queen's Bench Division is the division dealing with the majority of cases involving breach of contract and actions in tort (*e.g.* negligence, defamation, nuisance etc.).

Writs may be issued out of the High Court Central Office in London, or from any of the 130 or so provincial offices of the High Court (referred to as District Registries) throughout England and Wales.

In certain cases there is a jurisdictional overlap between cases which can be dealt with by the County Court and the High Court, but there are many matters for which the High Court has exclusive jurisdiction. As mentioned in paragraph C of this Chapter, there are limits placed on the jurisdiction of the County Court, but the High Court has no such limits.

Most actions commenced in the Queen's Bench Division are started by a writ. Writ forms are available from law stationers.

If you are bringing proceedings (plaintiff) you must either endorse a "statement of claim" on the writ itself or serve on the party you are suing (defendant) a separate statement of claim at any time up to 14 days after the acknowledgement of service (see later). A writ indorsed with a "statement of claim" is commonly referred to as a "specially indorsed writ". If it is not specially indorsed, the writ must contain a concise statement of the nature of your claim, commonly referred to as a "general indorsement", in which case the statement of claim must be served separately.

The writ is issued when it is sealed, that is stamped with the Court seal by the clerk at the Court Office. At least three writ forms are required, together with the appropriate fee, and all three forms are sealed. The writ will indicate the names of the plaintiff and the defendant, particulars of the claim and the Division of the High Court in which the proceedings are commenced. At least one form must be signed by you or your solicitor, and the signed copy is retained at the Court Office. The remaining two sealed copies will be returned to you, one for you to retain (called the original writ), the other to be served on the defendant. There is no need for you to attend at the Court Office in person, as writs may be issued by post.

You would be ill-advised to commence any action in the High Court without seeking the help of a solicitor. It is rare for an individual to conduct his own proceedings in the High Court. Bearing this in mind the further steps required are as follows:

Service of Writ

A writ is valid for service for 12 months from the date of issue, although if you have an adequate explanation for being unable to serve it within that period, you can apply for it to be renewed.

You must serve a sealed copy of the writ on the defendant, or on his solicitor if he is authorised to accept service. Service may be effected either in person or by post.

The writ served on the defendant must be accompanied by a form of acknowledgement of service.

Acknowledgement of Service

This will be the first step taken by the defendant. He is required to complete the form of acknowledgement of service and return it to the Court Office within 14 days after service of the writ. The Court staff will send you a copy of it. If the defendant fails to acknowledge service, you can obtain judgment against him. If he intends to defend, he is required to give you "notice of intention to defend" which he does by completing the relevant section of the acknowledgement of service form. You are entitled to judgment if he fails to give notice of intention to defend.

Pleadings

These are the formal documents by which the parties to the proceedings state their claims and defences. Your pleading as Plaintiff is called the "statement of claim" and, as previously mentioned, is either indorsed on the writ itself, or is served separately at any time up to 14 days after the acknowledgement of service. The defendant's pleading is called the "defence" and he is allowed a minimum of 28 days after service of the writ, in which to serve his defence. In addition to his defence, the defendant may file a counter claim.

Close of Pleadings

Pleadings are deemed to be closed 14 days after the last pleading was served. The last pleading may be the "defence", your "reply to defence", or your "reply to defence and counterclaim".

Discovery

This is the stage of an action commenced by writ, at which each party has to make and serve on his opponent a list of all the documents he has, or has had in his possession which are relevant to the case. Automatic discovery occurs within 14 days after the close of pleadings.

Having served your list of documents on the Defendant,

he must be given an opportunity within 7 days of service, to inspect the documents. There may be some documents which are not open to inspection, because they are "privileged". For example, confidential communications between a solicitor and his client.

For the purposes of obtaining evidence, automatic discovery is a very important stage in the proceedings, in that it enables the parties to assess the strengths and weaknesses of the documentary evidence.

Summons for Directions

This is a procedure which enables both the Court and the parties to the action, to take a thorough appraisal of the action. With notable exceptions, a summons for directions must be issued, usually by the plaintiff, within one month of the close of pleadings, and the parties are summoned to attend before the Master in Chambers. At this stage, the Master gives directions for any further preparations which may be necessary, and deals with the time, place and mode of trial. One notable exception to this procedure, is in most personal injury actions, where the Court gives automatic directions, so neither party is required to take out a summons for directions.

It is open to either party to apply for directions in addition to, or in variation of the automatic directions.

The Trial

High Court trials are normally dealt with by a single judge, as juries in civil courts are extremely rare.

The proceedings will be opened by Counsel (Barrister) for the Plaintiff, by outlining the facts. He will then call his first witness (usually the Plaintiff) who will be examined, cross-examined by Counsel for the Defence, and if necessary re-examined by Counsel for the Plaintiff. This procedure is repeated for all of the Plaintiff's witnesses.

Counsel for the Defence will open his case and call witnesses who will be examined etc., in the same way.

At the conclusion of the evidence, Counsel for the

Defence and then Counsel for the Plaintiff make closing speeches. It is open to Counsel for the Defence to submit that there is no case to answer, but if he makes such a submission, he is usually barred from calling evidence if it fails.

Judgment

After the closing speeches the judge will deliver his judgment. If there is a money judgment, there may be an application for interest made by the successful advocate, who will also ask for costs. High Court money judgments are usually payable forthwith.

The advocate for the unsuccessful party may apply for a "stay of execution" that is, an order preventing the successful party enforcing the order for payment. Such an application may be made if an appeal is pending, or if the loser is unable to pay. In the latter case the debtor must disclose to the Court his financial position, and if it is such that he cannot afford to pay the judgment debt in a lump sum, he will be ordered to pay by instalments.

E. SECRETARY OF STATE

Public concern for such matters as airport construction or extension, nuclear power stations and new coal mining operations, has resulted in protracted public inquiries. Here we are concerned primarily with those inquiries and appeals resulting from proposals more frequently occurring. Proposals which may affect you and your immediate environs include the erection, conversion or change of use of buildings, new roads, compulsory purchase orders, etc.

An inquiry is not a court of law, though its hearings are conducted on similar lines with regard to procedure and examination of witnesses. The main difference lies in there being no immediate judgment given at its conclusion, with neither fines nor terms of imprisonment being imposed on either party.[1]

---

[1] Except in the case of frivolous or vexatious objections, interference with witnesses and perjury.

Planning

If you have applied for planning permission for new buildings or works,[1] or for the change of use of existing buildings,[2] and the local council have refused to grant permission or have imposed unacceptable conditions, then you may appeal to the Secretary of State, Department of the Environment.[3] If the matter cannot be settled by the agreed submission of written representations to the Department of the Environment, a local public inquiry will be held.[4] The appeal decision is final whether following a public inquiry or the submission of written representations, and the only appeal then is to the High Court.[5]

Compulsory Purchase

Where a local council wish to make an Order for Compulsory Purchase, they are required to bring the matter to the attention of persons residing in the area. This is achieved by posting copies of a notice in the area affected, and by the publication of public notices in newspapers circulating in the area.

These notices will state:

(*a*) the title of the Order, and that it has been made by resolution of the council having been signed and sealed accordingly.

(*b*) that a copy of the Order and any relevant map or schedule is available for public inspection at specified times and places.

(*c*) the name and address of the person to whom objections should be addressed.

(*d*) the period during which objections will be received.

On receipt of objections the Secretary of State may decide to hold either a hearing or a formal local public inquiry.

---

[1] T.C.P.A. 1971, s. 22(1).
[2] Includes land.
[3] T.C.P.A. 1971, s. 36(1).
[4] T.C.P.A. 1971, s. 36(4).
[5] Within 6 weeks of the decision.

Making Objections

There are no prescribed forms for objections, though your letter of objection should include your name and address, the title of the order and the grounds of your appeal. It is important that your objections should relate directly to the effect of the order in question and not allude to the alleged undesirable consequences of such orders generally.

It is also worthwhile seeking professional advice if you consider appearing at an inquiry, if only in the preparation of statements, as the presentation of coherent documents, suitably cross-referenced and indexed will make the Inspector's task much lighter.

You can withdraw an objection by writing to the Secretary of State in a similar way, though in the case of a withdrawal too late to prevent the holding of an inquiry, you may be liable for costs.

You will be notified by the Secretary of State of the date, time and venue of the inquiry, and the local council will also advertise the arrangements.

You may be represented by legal advisors or appear on your own behalf, though financial assistance towards legal representation is not given.

Conduct of the Inquiry

An Inspector is appointed by the Secretary of State to conduct the inquiry and report back to him. He is usually well versed in the matter of dispute though he may sit with technical advisors. His duties are:

(*a*) to see that anyone having an interest has a fair opportunity of presenting a case for or against the proposal.

(*b*) to record the relevant facts.

(*c*) to report back to the Secretary of State:

(*i*) presenting his views on the relevant merits of the arguments for and against the proposal.

(*ii*) recommending whether or not the proposal or order should be confirmed.

The procedure is not governed by statutory rules and the Inspector conducts the inquiry at his discretion. The usual format is as follows:

(*a*) After opening the inquiry, he may discuss procedural arrangements with objectors' representatives, with regard to the order in which objectors are to be heard, and to assess the amount of time required for the inquiry. Thereafter, he generally takes a low profile adopting a listening approach, and occasionally querying statements in order to resolve any ambiguity, or bringing the inquiry to order.

(*b*) The case for the local council is presented. Witnesses are examined on their written statements, cross-examined by objectors or their representatives, and at the discretion of the inspector, they may be re-examined.

(*c*) The case for the objectors is presented with the same examination of witnesses by the local council's representative.

(*d*) The local council's representative may then be invited to clear up any remaining points.

(*e*) The inspector announces his intention to visit the area or place of the order in question, at a particular time.

The Decision

The Secretary of State makes his decision taking the inspector's recommendations into account, but not being bound by them. The order may be confirmed with or without modifications or rejected. If confirmed, the order becomes operative on the date specified. As far as costs are concerned, each side normally pays its own, but the Secretary of State has the discretion to order one party to bear all or part of the other's costs. In practice, this is only done where a party is found to have behaved unreasonably, vexatiously or frivolously.

Appeals

You may apply to the High Court, questioning the validity of the Secretary of State's decision, if you feel that he has exceeded his powers under the statute in question.

If dissatisfied with the conduct of the inquiry, you may send details to the Council on Tribunals within whose jurisdiction such matters fall. The Council on Tribunals would not concern themselves however with the merits of the decision, having no powers to change it.

Offences at Inquiries

Protection of witnesses is afforded in giving evidence to a Royal Commission, a committee of either House of Parliament or other public inquiry. It is an offence to threaten punish, damnify or injure such a witness, and the penalty is a fine on summary conviction.[1]

It is an offence, knowingly or wilfully to make a statement or oral declaration which is false in any material particular. The penalty on summary conviction is a fine or imprisonment.[2]

F. OMBUDSMAN

Complaints have no doubt been made about injustice ever since the first Local Boards of Health were established in the latter part of the nineteenth century. It was only following local government reorganisation in 1974, that a formal complaints procedure was established.[3]

If you consider that you have suffered injustice because of maladministration by a local council, police or water authority, you may complain to the Local Commissioner for Administration (the Ombudsman) in order to have the matter investigated.

Maladministration covers the administrative action (or

[1] W(PI)PA 1892, s. 3, as amended by the C.A. 1971, Schd. 8.
[2] P.A. 1911, s. 5, false declarations without oath.
[3] L.G.A. 1974.

inaction) or conduct of the local council, police or water authority, and may include arbitrariness, malice, bias, unfair discrimination, neglect, unjustifiable delay, incompetence, failure to observe rules or procedures etc.

The following paragraphs relate to the making of a complaint against a local council:

Making a Complaint

The Commissioner can only investigate a complaint after it has been brought to the attention of the council, and they have had the opportunity to reply. If the council department concerned fails to respond, then you should approach an elected member, with a request that your complaint be forwarded to the Ombudsman. Only if the member fails to refer the matter, can you write to the Commissioner direct.

It may seem that natural justice is not perpetrated when you have to elicit the support of a member of the same council against which you wish to complain. This requirement, however, ensures that the complaint is raised at councillor level, and gives the council the opportunity of rectifying the matter, thus avoiding what would otherwise be a time consuming and expensive investigation.

The written complaint should include your name; address; name of the council or authority complained against; details of your complaint; how you have previously brought your complaint to the attention of the council; letters or copy letters you wish to submit in support; date on which the action complained of took place; name or title of any officer or member you wish to complain about (with reasons); a request for a member of the authority to refer the matter to the Local Commissioner; your signature and date.

Investigation

The Commissioner will examine your complaint to see whether it is within his scope. Before starting his investigation the Commissioner will notify both you and the local member, whether or not he has accepted the complaint for investigation. The council or authority will then be notified, together with any officer or member named, and given the opportunity to comment on the allegations.

On completion of the investigation, the Commissioner will send you a report of his findings, copies of which will also be sent to the authority and any official or member named in the complaint.

It may be necessary for the Commissioner to visit you or ask you to attend for interview, in order to obtain further information, though all investigations are conducted in private. The Commissioner has wide powers to inspect the council's internal documents and to take written and oral evidence from any person whom he considers able to provide relevant details.

Reports

The Commissioner's report must be made freely available by the investigated authority, for at least three weeks following its publication. The council will announce by public notice that the report has been received, and give details as to when and where a copy can be seen. Where maladministration has been found the council must duly consider the report and inform the Commissioner what action they propose to take to resolve the matter.

Matters which will not be investigated

The Commissioner has no power to investigate matters relating to action taken before 1st April, 1974, or any grievances the subject of a tribunal, Ministerial inquiry or before a court of law. If you have a right of appeal or remedy through the courts and have not used it, he may not accept the complaint for investigation.

The Commissioner will not investigate matters which affect all or a large number of inhabitants of the area against say, the general level of rates.

Other matters excluded from investigation include: civil or criminal proceedings; investigation or prevention of crime; personnel matters within the authority or council;

teaching methods and organisation of schools; the commercial transactions of any authority.

G. RENT TRIBUNAL

This is one of the statutory tribunals[1] which is subject to the scrutiny of the Council on Tribunals whose members are appointed by the Lord Chancellor.[2]

Tribunals have played an increasingly important role in administrative and judicial matters, having the advantages of comparative speed, cheapness and informality. They are composed of members of the legal profession, judges and expert laymen. Tribunals are obliged to observe natural justice, and appeals on points of law or jurisdiction are heard by the High Court.[3]

For practical purposes, Rent Assessment Committees now carry out the functions of Rent Tribunals in relation to disputes over "regulated tenancy" rents, and change their name to Rent Tribunals when exercising their jurisdiction relating to "restricted contract" lettings.[4]

Making an appeal

To bring a case before a Rent Assessment Committee or Tribunal, you should obtain the required form from the Rent Officer. Details of your name; address; name and address of your landlord; particulars of the matters appealed against; grounds of the appeal; are required.

Procedure

This is similar to that of a public inquiry except that it is not public. The hearing is informal and in addition to the tribunal itself, those present will only include you and the other party and your legal representatives, if any.

---

[1] Others include: Lands Tribunals, Mental Health Review Tribunals, Income Tax Tribunals, Industrial Tribunals, Criminal Injuries Compensation Tribunals.

[2] T.I.A. 1971, ss. 7, 2(1).

[3] T.I.A. 1971, s. 13. Divisional Court, Queen's Bench Division.

[4] H.A. 1980, s. 72.

The conduct of the hearing is at the discretion of the Chairman in relation to the giving of evidence and examination of witnesses. After having heard both sides, the Chairman will usually give the Committee or Tribunal's decision. Either party may apply for the decision to be reviewed, and appeals to the High Court may be made on points of law, but the High Court will not review the rent fixed by the Committee.

The Rent Assessment Committee will review the rent determined by the rent officer, but they will not necessarily decide in favour of the person who objects. The committee may approve the Rent Officer's assessment or fix a higher or lower figure.

Appeals cannot be brought where the landlord has obtained a Certificate of Fair Rent, and the rent registered is the same as in the certificate, or where the Rent Officer registers a rent on joint application of landlord and tenant.

H. LANDS TRIBUNAL

The Lands Tribunal[1] is constituted on similar lines to a Rent Tribunal and is subject to the same rules.

You may appeal to the Lands Tribunal if you require amongst other things, adjudication on valuation for compulsory purchase or the waiving of restrictive covenants. For matters concerned with valuation or compensation, the Lands Tribunal sits as a Leasehold Valuation Tribunal, which is a Rent Assessment Committee under another name.[2]

Application

You may apply to the Leasehold Valuation Tribunal on the prescribed form.[3] The conduct of the hearing is for practical purposes the same as for Rent Tribunals or Rent Assessment Committees.

---

[1] Created under the L.T.A. 1949, s. 1.
[2] H.A. 1980, s. 142(2).
[3] H.A. 1980, Schd. 22, para. 8(2).

With the consent of the claimant in compensation cases, the Tribunal may determine applications on the basis of written representations. This negates the need for attendance of yourself, your landlord, legal advisors and witnesses, saving time and money as a result.

Appeals

If you are aggrieved by the decision of a Leasehold Valuation Tribunal, you may appeal to the Lands Tribunal,[1] but you cannot appeal to the High Court on points of law, as you can from Rent Assessment Committees.[2]

I. VALUATION OFFICER (Rating)

Where the value of your property is significantly affected by nearby development or the activities of an adjacent occupier, you are entitled to apply for alteration of the "valuation list".[3] The usual intention of the householder is to secure a reduction in rateable value, and the amount of rates to be paid as a result.

Rates are now levied by two authorities, although some tenants will pay their rates as part of an inclusive rent.[4]

As an owner-occupier you will receive a "general rate" demand (including County and Parish precepts) which is intended along with direct government grants and other forms of income, to pay for local, county and parish council services. You will also receive a "sewerage and water rate" demand from your regional water authority, the purpose of which is self explanatory.

The "rateable value" of your property is based on a theoretical annual "**rentable**" value, assuming your house could be let on the open property market. The amount of rates you pay is the rateable value, multiplied by a "rate in

---

[1] H.A. 1980, Schd. 22, para. 2.
[2] T.I.A. 1971, s. 13(1), Schd. 1, para. 28.
[3] G.R.A. 1967, ss. 19–25.
[4] G.R.A. 1967, s. 55.

the pound". If your rateable value is say £300, and the rate in the pound £1.50, then the demand would be for £450.

Appeals

You have a right of appeal against the rate demand to the Crown Court, except on matters of valuation.[1] Until the appeal is determined, the local council are restricted in enforcing the demand.

If, as is more likely, you wish to have the valuation amended in your favour, you should obtain the necessary form, "proposal for alteration of the valuation list" from the District Valuation Office whose address will be in your telephone directory. The form requires: your name and full address, nature of the alteration you require, grounds for the proposed alteration, name of occupier, name of owner, date and signature.

The alteration you require may simply be "a reduction in rateable value" and the grounds could be any matters which are likely to affect the value of your property. For example: "my neighbour keeps goats in his garden, which is in close proximity to my house. The smell and noise from the property in my opinion depreciates the value of my house, and I am likely to suffer a loss on the sale."

If the valuation officer objects to your proposal, a copy of which is sent to the local council as rating authority, the matter will be listed for hearing at the Valuation Court. The hearing is informal, and would be conducted on similar lines to a Rent Assessment Committee.

If you are aggrieved by a decision of the Valuation Court, you have a right of appeal to the Lands Tribunal, and from there to the Court of Appeal, on a point of law.

If the Valuation Officer and the local council agree not to object to your proposal, your claim would be known as "well founded", and a three party agreement form would be issued for signature by you, the council and the valuation officer, subject to agreement on the scale of alteration.

[1] G.R.A. 1967, s. 7, as amended.

Certain matters might be agreed before the proposal reaches Valuation Court stage. If there has been an error in assessment, for example, where your house has been valued as a "house and garage", and the garage does not exist, or, where your property is served by a cesspool and the valuation is based on mains drainage, then your proposal would be well founded.

A temporary reduction in valuation may be achieved where a new estate has been constructed, and the roads and street lighting remain unfinished. If such works are not complete within two years of your taking up occupation, then you would be entitled to a reduction in valuation, until they are finished.

The valuation of your house will be increased where you build extensions or carry out substantial improvements.

PART II

THE LEGAL RESPONSIBILITIES OF HOUSEHOLDERS

CHAPTER 6

ACCESS AND LIABILITY

A. RIGHTS OF ENTRY

A significant number of authorised personnel may require access to your home, normally after giving notice of their intention, but exceptionally without giving such notice.

Powers of entry are direct negations of the rights of private persons as established in common law, and should therefore be used judiciously, tactfully and strictly for the purposes for which they are given.

Public Health

An authorised officer[1] of the local council has, on producing if required a duly authenticated document showing his authority, a right to enter your home at all reasonable hours.[2] The right may be exercised for any of the following purposes; to ascertain

(*a*) whether or not there is or has been any contravention of the provisions of the Public Health Acts, or byelaws or Building Regulations made under them.

(*b*) whether or not circumstances exist which would justify taking any action or executing any works.

and for the purposes of:

---

[1] Defined in P.H.A. 1936, s. 343.
[2] P.H.A. 1936, s. 287, as amended by P.H.A. 1961, Schd. 1 Part 3.

(*a*) taking such action or executing such works authorised by the Acts, Byelaws or Regulations.

(*b*) performing their functions under the Acts generally.

Entry cannot be demanded as of right, unless you have been given twenty-four hours notice of the intended entry.

If admission has been or is likely to be refused, a justice of the peace, on sworn information in writing, may by warrant authorise the local council or its authorised officer(s) to enter, if need be by force. You must be given notice of the intention to apply for a warrant, unless the giving of such notice would defeat the object of entry.[1] The penalty for obstruction is a fine on summary conviction.[2]

Housing

Any person authorised in writing, stating the purposes for which entry is authorised by the local council, may at all reasonable times enter your house, premises or buildings.[3] You must be given twenty-four hours notice, as should the owner of the property.

Entry would be valid for the following purposes:

(*a*) survey or valuation for compulsory purchase.

(*b*) survey and examination in connection with service of a notice requiring repair.

(*c*) survey and examination in connection with a closing or demolition order.

(*d*) measurement of rooms in order to determine whether or not the house is overcrowded.

The penalty for obstruction is a fine on summary conviction.[4]

---

[1] Or where the premises are unoccupied, or access is required in an emergency.
[2] P.H.A. 1936, s. 288, as amended by P.H.A. 1961, Schd. 1 Part 3.
[3] H.A. 1957, s. 159, as amended by L.G.A. 1972, Schd. 30.
[4] H.A. 1957, s. 161, as amended.

Electricity

An Electricity Board may by notice in writing require you, within a reasonable time after service of the notice, to permit an officer or servant of the Board to enter your premises. The officer or servant must be duly authorised by them in writing, and may inspect and test your installation at any time between the hours of 9.00 am and 6.00 pm.[1]

Notice may be served under these provisions if the Electricity Board have reasonable grounds for supposing that:—

(*a*) a leakage exceeding the "specified amount"[2] exists, **or**

(*b*) your installation or any part of it fails to satisfy the requirements of the Regulations.[3]

If you refuse admission, the Board may seek a warrant, granted by a justice of the peace, to authorise such entry if need be by force.[4] Before granting a warrant, the justice of the peace must be satisfied that:—

(*a*) admission is reasonably required;

(*b*) that the Board or their employee is entitled to exercise a right of entry; **and**

(*c*) that the requirements of the Electricity Acts have been complied with (in regard to the service of notice etc.).

In any circumstances where the Board consider that immediate action is necessary in the interests of public safety, or to avoid undue interference with the supply to other consumers, they may immediately terminate your supply.[5] It is unlikely that any emergency would justify the invasion of your home, but if such circumstances arose and you refused access to the Board's officers, they could term-

---

[1] Electricity Supply Regulations, 1937, Reg. 32(a)(ii).

[2] The "specified amount" is one ten thousandth (0.0001) part of the maximum current supplied.

[3] Electricity Supply Regulations, 1937, Regs. 27–31 inclusive.

[4] RE(GAEB)A 1954, s. 2.

[5] Electricity Supply Regulations, 1937, Reg. 32(a)(i).

inate your supply by breaking into the service line outside your boundary, or obtain a warrant to effect entry.

In this case, a justice of the peace must be satisfied before granting the warrant, that either:—

(*a*) a minimum of twenty four hours' notice of the intended entry had been given, **or**

(*b*) admission was sought and refused in an emergency, **or**

(*c*) the premises are unoccupied, **or**

(*d*) a request for admission would defeat the object of entry.[1]

If the Electricity Board enter premises by warrant where the occupier is temporarily absent or where the premises are unoccupied, they are obliged to leave them as secure against trespass as they were when they entered.[2]

The penalty for obstructing an authorised officer in possession of a warrant, would render you liable to a fine.

It should be remembered that the service line and primary meter are the property of the Electricity Board, and you will probably have signed an "Application for a Supply of Electricity" when taking up residence. On signing the form you will have agreed to be bound by the Board's conditions, the Electricity Acts, Regulations and Orders currently in force, requiring you amongst other things to give access for maintenance of the Board's equipment.

Gas

An officer duly authorised by the Gas Region may at all reasonable times, on production of an authenticated document showing his authority, enter your premises for the purposes of:—

(*a*) inspecting any service pipe, meters and fittings, **or**

---

[1] RE(GAEB)A, 1954, s. 2(2).
[2] RE(GAEB)A, 1954, s. 2(5).

(*b*) ascertaining the quantity of gas consumed (except where disconnection has been requested by the occupier, and the Gas Region have failed to respond within a reasonable time)[1]

Except in cases of emergency, entry cannot be effected without your consent, unless a warrant has been obtained from a justice of the peace.[2]

You would be entitled to twenty four hours' notice in writing, if the Gas Region require access for the purposes of:—

(*a*) removing pipes, meters and fittings where you do not require a supply of gas, **or**

(*b*) disconnection (*i.e.* for non-payment of bills)[3]

Refusal of admission would not constitute an offence unless the person requiring admission had obtained a warrant to authorise entry,[4] when the penalty for obstruction would be a fine on summary conviction.

Powers of entry are also given to authorised officers, together with such other persons as may be necessary for:—

(*a*) inspecting any gas fitting, flue, means of ventilation, service pipe or other apparatus.

(*b*) examining or testing any such objects for compliance with thc Regulations,[5] or to ascertain whether or not such apparatus is likely to constitute a danger to any person or property, **and**

(*c*) where the officers consider a danger to life or property exists, they may disconnect and seal off any fitting or part of the supply system, or cut off the supply to the premises.[6]

---

[1] G.A. 1972, Schd. 4, para 24.
[2] RE(GAEB)A, 1954, s. 1(1). See p. 109 for conditions relating to the issue of warrants, where Gas=Electricity.
[3] G.A. 1972, Schd. 4, para 25(1).
[4] RE(GAEB)A, 1954, s. 1(3).
[5] Gas Safety Regulations, 1972, (S.I. 1972 No. 1178).
[6] Gas Safety (Rights of Entry) Regulations, 1983, (S.I. 1983 No. 1575).

In cases of emergency, entry can be effected without notice, your consent or a warrant. In any other circumstances your consent or a warrant of a justice of the peace is required.[1] The penalty for obstruction of an officer who requires admission by warrant, is a fine on summary conviction.

Any person who enters premises under the authority of a warrant, and the premises are unoccupied or the occupier is temporarily absent, is obliged to leave the premises as secure against trespassers as when he found them.[2]

Water

In the detection of waste or misuse of water, an authorised officer of the water authority may enter your premises, if supplied by them, between the hours of 7 a.m. and one hour after sunset. If after producing his written authority, you refuse him admission, you will commit an offence and be liable to a fine on summary conviction.[3]

Entry cannot be demanded as of right for the purposes of installing, connecting, disconnecting, examining or reading meters, unless you have been given twenty-four hours notice.[4] If entry is still refused, then a justice of the peace may authorise entry by warrant.

The penalty for obstruction is a fine on summary conviction.[5]

B. OCCUPIERS' LIABILITY

Safety of Visitors

The responsibility for personal injury or damage extends to all occupiers.

A common duty of care is owed to everyone who enters

---

[1] RE(GAEB)A, 1954, s. 1(1)
[2] RE(GAEB)A, 1954, s. 2(5)
[3] W.A. 1945, Schd. 3, para. 62.
[4] W.A. 1973, s. 32(3).
[5] W.A. 1973, s. 32(8).

your house, even to trespassers in some circumstances. By definition, the duty is "to take such care as in all the circumstances of the case is reasonable, to see that the visitor will be reasonably safe in using the premises for the purposes for which he is invited or permitted to be there."[1]

A breach of this duty, which demands a higher standard of care in respect of children, may result in a claim for damages against you where negligence has resulted in injury or death.

Those persons to whom you give invitation or permission to enter your house, or use it, are visitors. Those entrants whom you might regard as trespassers are protected by common law rules. If an entrant does not use your premises for the purpose for which he has been given permission to enter, you do not owe him the same "duty of care", and his rights are limited to those of a trespasser in common law.

Authorised officers of local councils, gas regions, electricity boards, water authorities, police authorities etc., are, if duly authorised by statute, to be treated as having been given permission to be on your premises, even though you have not invited or permitted them to enter. As a result the statutory duty of care is owed, whether they have your permission to be there or not.

In establishing the **degree of care** owed to your visitor, and the degree of care which the visitor can be expected to exercise, the following are to be considered:

(*a*) an occupier must be prepared for children to be less careful than adults, and,

(*b*) an occupier may expect a visitor to appreciate and guard against any special risks attached to the reason for his visit, when left free to do so by the occupier.[2]

---

[1] O.L.A. 1957, s. 2(2).
[2] O.L.A. 1957, s. 2(3).

Children

In deciding whether or not a danger exists, you must have regard to the physical and mental powers of the child visitor. A child may be susceptible to allurement or temptation, and may or may not be accompanied by an adult. Your local council has a duty of care in respect of swings, slides and roundabouts etc., on a children's playground.

Warnings

The issue of a warning can only discharge your liability if it is sufficient in all the circumstances to enable the visitor to be reasonably safe.[1] You do not have any obligations to visitors in respect of risks willingly accepted,[2] but the visitors knowledge of the danger does not necessarily discharge you from liability. It depends on whether or not this knowledge is in all the circumstances sufficient to enable him to be reasonably safe.

Until 1978, occupiers were permitted to limit their liability, by, for example, displaying notices excluding their liability. However, exclusions of this kind are now void in respect of any claim for death or personal injury, where the duty arises from things done in the course of a business, or from the occupation of business premises.[3]

Trespassers

The duty of care which you owe, is a lower standard than that provided in the "duty of care" mentioned above and is limited to a common law "humanitarian" duty, to act in a humane manner according to common standards of civilised behaviour.

The duty of care is owed only to those trespassers whose presence you know of, or whose presence you might reasonably expect. Child trespassers who enter your land and climb on structures are owed a higher standard of care, in

[1] O.L.A. 1957, s. 2(4)(a).
[2] O.L.A. 1957, s. 2(5).
[3] U.C.T.A. 1977, s. 2. Operative date 1.2.78.

particular where an allurement, *i.e.* an attractive object is left in such a place where children are known to play.

You may neglect a bare possibility that trespassers may enter your land, but you have a duty when you know of facts which indicate a substantial likelihood that they may enter. The common law duty to trespassers is perhaps best illustrated by a decision of the House of Lords,[1] where the defendants owned an electrified railway line which was fenced off from a meadow where children lawfully played. The defendants knew that the fence was delapidated and that children played on the line, but they did not repair the fence. The six year old plaintiff walked over the broken fence, trespassed on the railway track and was severely burned by the live line. The House unanimously held the defendants liable.

Repair and Maintenance

Landlord, tenant and owner-occupier may have liability for injury resulting from a failure to carry out their obligations to repair property. Your landlord may have a reasonable excuse, if he has no reason to know of, or has not been informed of the need for repair.

If you lend a neighbour scaffolding to enable him to paint his house, you will not be liable under the statutes for any injury he sustains in its use, but you may be liable under common law based on a duty owed in respect of its free hire, if known by you to be faulty.

On the other hand if you erect scaffolding for a contractor to work on your house, you would have sufficient control of it, to make you exercise a common duty of care, provided for by the Act.[2]

C. CONTRACTORS' LIABILITY

To a certain extent, the terms of a contract agreed between you and a contractor dictate who is responsible for

---

[1] *British Railways Board v. Herrington* [1972] 1 All E.R. 749, H.L.
[1] O.L.A. 1957, s. 1.

what. The contractor cannot, however, discharge himself from responsibility for injury or damage, where the statutes have laid down specific rules, or where common law duties exist.

The statutory duty of care is owed by persons who build or convert your house, in respect of injuries resulting from any failure to carry out their work in a workmanlike or professional manner, and with proper materials.[1] Any person you employ to carry out works or services, is obliged to conduct his activities so as not to expose himself or you to a risk to your health and safety.[2]

Whenever a contractor or landlord installs appliances or executes works of repair, his liability will depend on the extent to which you as an injured party, could have known of any inherent dangers. The contractor's liability for negligence in relation to his activities on land has been considered by the House of Lords in a case[3] where B. Ltd., building contractors, were employed to make alterations to the front part of a house. In the course of this work B. Ltd. failed to take reasonable care to make access to the house safe: in consequence R, a visitor, was injured when leaving the house during the hours of darkness. B. Ltd. were liable in negligence.

If you employ an independent contractor who you have reason to believe is competent, and he carries out his work improperly, then you may not be liable as an occupier for injury to visitors. Where danger exists due to faulty construction, maintenance or repair, you are not liable if you have acted reasonably in entrusting the work to him,[4] and provided that you took such steps (if any) as were reasonably necessary to ensure that the work was properly carried out.

---

[1] D.P.A. 1972, s. 1(1).
[2] H.S.W.A. 1974, s. 3(2).
[3] *A.C. Billings & Sons Ltd. v. Riden* [1957] 3 All E.R. 1, H.L.
[4] O.L.A. 1957, s. 2(4)(b).

Visiting Workers

A window cleaner can be expected to guard against the special risks attached to his occupation. If your house is in some obvious way defective, and the window sill or frame used for a handhold fails, then you may not be liable for any injury sustained. On the other hand, if the window cleaner or chimney sweep falls in your home as a result of defective steps, then you may be liable.

As an occupier you would not be liable for injury to your domestic help, where a contractor puts in a new switch fuse, as you are entitled to trust the contractor.[1]

D. PERSONS A DANGER TO THEMSELVES

The local council may, on an order granted by a magistrates' court, remove you from your home to a hospital or other place, if:

(*a*) you are suffering from grave chronic disease or by virtue of age, infirmity or handicap you are living in insanitary conditions, **and**

(*b*) you are unable to give yourself proper care and attention, and there is no-one else to render such care.[2]

Application to the court would be in the form of a written certificate of the District Community Physician (formerly Medical Officer of Health) who may be required to give oral evidence. The District Community Physician must be satisfied after thorough inquiry, that such action is in your interests, and that it is necessary to prevent injury to your health or that of other persons who may be affected by serious nuisance.

The detention may not be for more than three months though the court may extend the period by order for a further three months.

---

[1] *Cook v. Broderip* (1968) 206 Estates Gazette. 128.

[2] N.A.A. 1948, s. 47, as amended.

CHAPTER 7

NUISANCE

You have rights and responsibilities in the creation of nuisance, both in common law (precedent) and statute law.[1] (Acts of Parliament)

A nuisance may be a civil wrong (a tort) and/or a criminal act, and in the vast majority of cases involves an interference with the use and enjoyment of land. Such interferences can be created by water, fire, smoke, smell, fumes, gas, noise, heat, electricity, disease, obstruction, dangerous acts and matters which are prejudicial to health.

The action which you may take to resolve a nuisance depends on the category within which the "act or omission" falls, and whether you are the sole victim or one of many.

A. PUBLIC NUISANCE

A public nuisance may be a criminal act, resulting in prosecution on indictment or summary proceedings, or a civil wrong where the remedy is a civil action for an injunction and/or damages.

The obstruction of a highway; interference with the navigation of a stream; pollution of the atmosphere with fumes; emission of noise from steam hammers or fairgrounds; keeping a brothel, etc., are matters which affect the public at large, and are potentially public nuisances. Some of these

[1] P.H.A. 1936, Part III.

may also be statutory nuisances, for which the local council has specific remedies.

The distinction between "public" and "private" nuisances depends on the number of persons affected in each case. In 1957, Lord Justice Denning said:[1]

> "I prefer to look at the reason of the thing, and to say that a public nuisance is a nuisance which is so widespread in its range or so indiscriminate in its effect, that it would not be reasonable to expect one person to take proceedings on his own to put a stop to it, but that it should be the responsibility of the public at large."

Once a public nuisance is proved, however, you could pursue a private action by way of a claim for damages. Such a claim need not be restricted to an actual financial loss, but may represent a loss due to substantial inconvenience or delay, provided that it is a loss appreciably greater than any suffered by the general public.

Probably the most common claim in public nuisance is for injuries to persons sustained when using the highway. If you fall over a projection on a public pavement, or, in avoiding an obstruction on a pavement deviate slightly from it and fall, both incidents may be pursued as public nuisance actions. If such a fall is on a shop forecourt, which is not part of the public footpath, then your claim would be for negligence against the proprietor.

A public nuisance may also arise in the obstruction of your access by erections on the highway, or by suffering damage as a result of nuisance on the highway.

B. PRIVATE NUISANCE

A person commits a private nuisance "when he is held to be responsible for an act indirectly causing physical injury to land, or substantially interfering with the use or enjoyment of land, or of an interest in land, where, in the light

---

[1] *Att.-Gen. v. P.Y.A. Quarries Ltd.* [1957] 2 Q.B. 169.

of all the surrounding circumstances, this injury or interference is held to be unreasonable."[1]

Where a neighbour's dog continually barks, or where an adjacent occupier plays his hi-fi system loudly and persistently, you may sue for damages and apply for an injunction restraining him from continuing the nuisance.[2]

Missiles in the form of golf balls, may strike you when lawfully using the highway, or in the "enjoyment" of your garden. Here again lies the distinction which can be drawn between "public" and "private" nuisance, and is further confirmed in the case of *Castle v. St. Augustine's Links Ltd.*[3] where the plaintiff, while using the highway was blinded by a golf ball driven from a tee on the defendants' adjoining course. He was held able to recover from the owners of the club for damages arising from *public* nuisance.

It follows then that the golf ball striking you on your garden would give rise to an action in private nuisance, and afford the ability to recover damages, or seek injunctive relief.

If the golf club had constructed the course, so that it was likely and foreseable that harm would come to occupiers or their property, then they would be liable in private nuisance for damage.

The degree of Interference

A Victorian Judge, Vice-Chancellor Knight-Bruce gave the following interpretation, which is still relied upon today:[4]

> "ought this inconvenience to be considered in fact as more than fanciful, more than one of mere delicacy or fastidiousness, as an inconvenience materially interfering with the ordinary comfort physically of human existence, not merely according to elegant or dainty modes and

---

[1] *Street on Torts*, Butterworth & Co. Ltd. 1976, p. 219.

[2] A much simpler remedy exists under the C.P.A. 1974, see Chapter 4, para. A, p. 64, but does not allow a damages claim.

[3] (1922) 38 T.L.R. 615.

[4] *Walter v. Selfe* (1851) 4 De G. & Sm. 315.

habits of living, but according to plain and sober and simple notions among the English people."

This material interference with ordinary physical comfort may amount to danger. It has been stated that:[1]

"private nuisance arises out of a state of things on one man's property whereby his neighbour's property is exposed to danger"

This ruling gives justification for regarding these matters as private nuisances, as the following cases illustrate:

Defective electrical wiring was installed in the defendant's premises. This caused a fire resulting in the destruction of the plaintiff's adjoining bungalow.[2]

In the case where a neighbour allowed a culvert to remain blocked so flooding another's adjoining land, it was said that it was a nuisance because:

"It created a state of things from which, when the ditch was flowing in full stream, an obstruction might reasonably be expected in the pipe, from which flooding might reasonably be expected to result."[3]

Reasonableness

It is appropriate here to consider what is meant by reasonableness, a term which is widely used in case and statute law.

When can you or your neighbour be "reasonably expected" to foresee the results of action or inaction? Who is a "reasonable man"?

The following case is not strictly applicable to private nuisance, but indicates a judicial interpretation of the standard of foresight which a reasonable man might be expected to have:

"the standard of foresight of the reasonable man is in one

---

[1] *Torette House Property Ltd. v. Berkman* (1939) 62 C.L.R. 637.
[2] *Spicer v. Smee* [1946] 1 All E.R. 489.
[3] *Sedleigh-Denfield v. O'Callaghan* [1940] 3 All E.R. 349 H.L.

sense an impersonal test. It limits the personal equation and is independent of the idiosyncrasies of the particular persons whose conduct is in question. Some persons are unduly timorous and imagine every path beset with lions; others, of more robust temperaments, fail to foresee or nonchalantly disregard even the most obvious dangers. The reasonable man is presumed to be free both from over-apprehension and from over-confidence."[1]

An action for private nuisance may not succeed solely on proving substantial interference, it is necessary to demonstrate that the interference results from unreasonable acts or omissions. Referring again to the case of *Sedleigh-Denfield v. O'Callaghan*, Lord Wright said:

"A balance has to be maintained between the right of the occupier to do what he likes with his own (land), and the right of his neighbour not to be interfered with. It is impossible to give any precise or universal formula, but it may broadly be said that a useful test is perhaps what is reasonable according to the ordinary usages of mankind living in society . . ."[2]

The act or omission resulting in private nuisance must be unreasonable in all the circumstances of the case. For example what may constitute a private nuisance in a peaceful rural setting, may not be so regarded in an urban environment. In 1863, Chief Justice Earle said:

"It seems to me that the affairs of life in a dense neighbourhood cannot be carried on without mutual sacrifices of comfort; and that, in all actions for discomfort, the law must regard the principle of mutual adjustment . . ."[3]

In 1879, it was further stated that:

"what would be a nuisance in Belgravia Square would not necessarily be so in Bermondsey . . ."[4]

Whilst locality is a factor when considering personal

[1] *Glasgow Corporation v. Muir* [1943] 2 All E.R. 44.
[2] [1940] 3 All E.R. 349 H.L.
[3] *Cavey v. Ledbitter* (1863) 13 C.B.N.S. 470.
[4] *Sturges v. Bridgman* (1879) 11 Ch.D. 852.

discomfort, it is not a factor when the nuisance is one which has caused physical injury to the plaintiff, or damage to his land. Other factors which might be taken into account by the Courts, where nuisance results in personal discomfort include malice, social utility and sensitivity.

C. STATUTORY NUISANCE

The Public Health Acts enumerate certain conditions which might ordinarily constitute common law nuisances, but which can nevertheless be dealt with summarily. (i.e. in a magistrate's court)

Your local council is obliged to inspect its area from time to time to detect the existence of "statutory nuisances" and to take action to see that they are abated.[1]

"Statutory Nuisance" is defined as something which either injures or is likely to injure health, or is a nuisance to the inhabitants of the neighbourhood and which admits of a remedy, either by the individual whose act or omission causes the nuisance, or by the local authority.

The principal category of statutory nuisances is listed in the Public Health Act, 1936,[2] and there are further matters in the Act which can be so regarded, as well as nuisances declared by other Acts to be statutory nuisances.

The first group are listed as follows:

(*a*) any premises in such a state as to be prejudicial to health or a nuisance.

(*b*) any animal kept in such a place or manner as to be prejudicial to health or a nuisance.

(*c*) any accumulation or deposit which is prejudicial to health or a nuisance.

(*d*) any dust or effluvia, caused by any trade, business, manufacture or process, which is injurious or likely to cause injury to the public health, or a nuisance.

---

[1] P.H.A. 1936, s. 91.

[2] P.H.A. 1936, s. 92(1) as amended.

(*e*) any workplace which is not provided and maintained with sufficient means of ventilation; not kept clean, free from noxious effluvia or is overcrowded. (summarised)

(*f*) any other matter declared by the Act, to be a statutory nuisance.

The "other matters" are as follows:

(*a*)(*i*) any pond, pool, ditch, gutter or watercourse which is so foul or in such a state as to be prejudicial to health or a nuisance.

(*ii*) any part of a watercourse which is so choked or silted up as to obstruct or impede the proper flow of water, causing a nuisance or giving rise to conditions prejudicial to health.[1]

(*b*) any tent, van, shed or similar structure used for human habitation which is in such a state, or is overcrowded, or by the absence of proper sanitary accommodation, gives rise to a nuisance or conditions prejudicial to health.[2]

(*c*) any storage container for water used for domestic purposes, so constructed or kept as to render the water liable to contamination, and to be prejudicial to health.[3]

Other Acts of parliament declaring some of their provisions to be statutory nuisances, govern the following matters:

(*a*) any shaft or outlet of an abandoned mine, not properly fenced so as to prevent any person from accidentally falling down it, or any unfenced quarry.[4]

(*b*) any smoke, other than from domestic chimneys or "dark smoke" from an industrial chimney, which is a

---

[1] P.H.A. 1936, s. 259(1).
[2] P.H.A. 1936, s. 268(2).
[3] P.H.A. 1936, s. 141.
[4] M.Q.A. 1954, s. 151.

nuisance to the inhabitants of the neighbourhood.[1] (*i.e.* bonfires)

There are in addition, other matters which are regarded as nuisances, but which are not "statutory" within the meaning of the Public Health Act 1936.

(*a*) any "barbed wire fence" adjoining a highway may be a nuisance.[2]

(*b*) any cesspool in such a condition as to be prejudicial to health or a nuisance.[3]

(*c*) any closets, in such a state as to be prejudicial to health or a nuisance.[4]

(*d*) any noise or vibration which is a nuisance.[5]

Before considering the procedure for abatement, the terms "nuisance" and "prejudicial to health" require explanation.

The term "prejudicial to health" is defined as "injurious or likely to cause injury to health".[6]

The word "nuisance" has, however, exercised the minds of many eminent judges. The view has been taken that where premises are in such a state as to interfere with the personal comfort of the occupiers, a statutory nuisance exists, regardless of whether the premises are prejudicial to health.

The particular case which gave rise to this position involved a landlord's attempt to harrass a tenant, who failed to pay his rent or abide with a notice to quit. The landlord removed the window sashes and a door. Chief Justice Caldecote said:

"If a thing is an interference with the comfort of persons, it will be a nuisance. Section 92 (of the 1936 Public Health

---

[1] C.A.A. 1956, s. 16.
[2] H.W.A. 1980, s. 164.
[3] P.H.A. 1936, s. 39(1)(c)
[4] P.H.A. 1936, s. 44(1)(b).
[5] C.P.A. 1974, s. 58.
[6] P.H.A. 1936, s. 343(1).

Act) goes a little further and makes it a statutory nuisance, so as to be capable of being remedied in a particular way, as provided for in Part III of the Act."[1]

The case established that both conditions of nuisance and prejudice to health need not exist, either being sufficient, if proved, to constitute a statutory nuisance.

However, the case's definition of nuisance was substantially altered by a more recent judgment. In 1976 it was held that "nuisance"[2] had the same meaning as public or private nuisance at common law, and that a statutory nuisance did not arise if the acts complained of, affected only the person occupying the premises where the nuisance allegedly took place.[3]

It should be clear then that a nuisance must affect other inhabitants of the neighbourhood to constitute a statutory nuisance.

Further cases have determined what may not be regarded as prejudicial to health or a nuisance. In *Springett v. Harold*,[4] the need for internal decorative repair in a house was not regarded as constituting a statutory nuisance, even though it caused discomfort and inconvenience. The courts have also held that dampness caused by condensation, where no structural defects exist, could not qualify as a nuisance, even if prejudicial to health.[5] In 1975, it was held that the visual impact of inert matter, arising from the dumping of household refuse and building materials, did not cause a nuisance. Inert matter cannot be prejudicial to health unless it causes a threat of disease or attracts vermin.[6]

Procedure

If the local council are satisfied that a statutory nuisance exists, they may serve an "abatement notice" on the person

---

[1] *Betts v. Penge Urban District Council*, [1942] 2 K.B. 154.
[2] In s. 92, P.H.A. 1936.
[3] *National Coal Board v. Thorne* [1976] 1 W.L.R. 543.
[4] [1954] 1 All E.R. 568.
[5] *Dover District Council v. Farrar & Others* [1980] 2 H.L.R. 32 D.C.
[6] *Coventry City Council v. Cartwright* [1975] 1 W.L.R. 845.

who causes it, or if that person cannot be found, on the relevant owner or occupier of the premises. The notice requires the nuisance to be abated, and specifies the necessary steps to achieve this. If the nuisance arises from a structural defect the notice must be served on the owner. If it is clear that the owner or occupier is not to blame, and the person responsible cannot be found, the council can abate the nuisance themselves.[1]

Failure to comply with the notice may result in the council applying to a magistrates' court for a "nuisance order", requiring the defendant to comply with the notice. The court may by order prohibit a recurrence of the nuisance, order its abatement and/or impose a fine. If the nuisance order is not complied with, the court may impose a further fine and a daily penalty for each day during which the nuisance continues. The council may carry out the specified works and recover their expenses "reasonably incurred".[2]

Appeals against abatement notices are considered in Chapter 5.

An application for a nuisance order may be made by any member of the public,[3] aggrieved by the nuisance.

If the council consider that their attempts to abate the nuisance under the above provisions would provide an inadequate remedy, they may take proceedings in the High Court, for abatement or prohibition of the nuisance.[4]

Other Remedies

In respect of **premises** prejudicial to health or a nuisance, where unreasonable delay would be incurred by following the 1936 Act procedure, the local council may serve a nine day notice.[5] The notice sets out the defects, and what the council proposes to do at the end of that period.

The recipient can serve a counter-notice within seven days

[1] P.H.A. 1936, s. 93.
[2] P.H.A. 1936, s. 95.
[3] P.H.A. 1936, s. 99.
[4] P.H.A. 1936, s. 100.
[5] P.H.A. 1961, s. 26.

announcing his intent to do the work. The council cannot then proceed, unless the work is not commenced within a reasonable period, or if started, little progress is made.

Recurring Nuisances

If the council are satisfied that a statutory nuisance has occurred and is likely to recur on the same premises, they may serve a prohibition notice.[1]

The notice prohibits the recurrence, and requires the person on whom it is served, to take such steps as may be necessary to that end.

Unlike the provisions mentioned earlier in this paragraph, a notice may be served whether or not the nuisance exists at the time of service, irrespective of service of an abatement notice.[2] The same document may contain a prohibition notice and an abatement notice.

[1] P.H.(RN)A. 1969, s. 1.
[2] Under s. 93 P.H.A. 1936.

CHAPTER 8

PETS

A. LICENSING

For the purposes of this book, I have confined the text to consideration of licensing of domestic pets. The licensing of riding establishments, pet shops, stallions etc., is dealt with comprehensively in *Animal Law*.[1]

Dogs

If your dog is over six months old, you are required to obtain a licence, usually from the post office, and pay the annual fee,[2] unless your dog is a guide dog[3] or a working dog on a farm.[4] The "**keeper**" of a dog is the person in whose charge, custody or possession it is, or in whose house or premises a dog is seen or found, in the absence of proof to the contrary.

If you do not have a licence, or fail to produce it to a police constable or an "authorised officer" of the council (a dog warden) within a reasonable time, you may be fined on summary conviction.

---

[1] By Godfrey Sandys-Winsch, published by Shaw & Sons Ltd.
[2] D.L.A. 1959, s. 1.
[3] D.L.A. 1959, s. 3.
[4] D.L.A. 1959, s. 4(1).

Your dog is required to have a collar, when in a public place, showing your name and address.[1]

Guard Dogs

It is not yet necessary to licence guard dogs, since those sections of the Act which governs these animals have not yet been brought into operation. Other provisions are, however, in force, the reason for which was a series of accidents in the mid 1970's.

If you keep a dog to protect your property, premises or to protect a person guarding them, you are obliged to secure it, so that it cannot roam the premises unless it is under the control of the handler.[2] The "handler" is defined as a person capable of controlling the dog.

You must also clearly exhibit a notice at each entrance to the premises, warning that a guard dog is present.[3]

If you keep a guard dog in contravention of the above rules, you commit an offence, which on summary conviction is punishable by fine.[4]

Dog Breeding

If you keep more than two breeding bitches, you are required to obtain a licence from the local council, and to pay the appropriate fee.[5] It is an offence to keep a breeding establishment without such a licence, and you may be fined on summary conviction.[6]

There is a right of appeal to a magistrates' court against the refusal of the local council to issue a licence.[7]

---

[1] Control of Dogs Order, 1930, (S.R. & O. 1930 No. 399 as amended by S.R. & O. 1930 No. 683; S.R. & O. 1931 No. 80) A.H.A. 1981, s. 13(2).
[2] G.D.A. 1975, s. 1, operative 1.2.76.
[3] G.D.A. 1975, s. 1(3).
[4] G.D.A. 1975, s. 5.
[5] B.D.A. 1973, s. 1(1).
[6] B.D.A. 1973, s. 1(9).
[7] B.D.A. 1973, s. 1(5).

Boarding

If you keep an animal boarding establishment, you are required to have a licence, which is issued by the local council on payment of the required fee.[1] They would need to be satisfied that your premises were suitable, and you would probably need planning permission for a "change of use".

An offence is committed by failing to be licensed, which is punishable by fine or imprisonment on summary conviction.[2] In addition you may be disqualified from keeping a boarding establishment for such period as the court may determine.

There is a right of appeal against the local council's refusal to issue a licence, to a magistrates' court.[3]

See also para. D, of this Chapter for the licensing of Dangerous Wild Animals.

Licensing Conditions

Before granting you a licence for dog breeding or animal boarding premises, the council need to be satisfied that certain conditions will be met. The standard conditions for both types of premises are broadly the same.

Animals must be suitably accommodated, fed, exercised and protected from disease and fire. If you keep a boarding establishment you must maintain a proper register of animals kept with their dates of arrival and departure, and their owners' names and addresses. A register is not required for a dog breeding establishment.

Authorised officers of the local council have powers of entry and inspection, at all reasonable hours, for securing compliance with the conditions. Offences are committed by wilfully obstructing or delaying these officers, and/or failing to comply with the conditions, which are punishable by fine on summary conviction.

---

[1] A.B.E.A. 1963, s. 1(1)(2).
[2] A.B.E.A. 1963, s. 3.
[3] A.B.E.A. 1963, s. 1(4).

B. DOG WARDENS

In an attempt to educate the less responsible pet owner, and reduce the numbers of strays in our towns and cities, some councils have appointed dog wardens, giving them the powers to seize, detain and dispose of stray dogs.[1]

Where such powers have not been obtained, the dog warden can still be effective, by acting in the capacity of an ordinary citizen in returning dogs to their owners or taking them to a police station.[2]

Where a dog has been seized, the owner must claim it within seven days paying any expenses involved in its keep, otherwise it may be destroyed.[3] A register must be maintained of all animals seized.

Justification for employing dog wardens, is also seen in the reduction of street accidents and fouling of footpaths. It is essential in carrying out his work, that the warden seeks the co-operation of the public, his first job being to return strays to their owners. If the owner cannot be found, or persistently or wilfully allows a dog to roam, then the warden takes the dog to the pound.

C. STRAY ANIMALS

Domestic pets have given rise to friction between neighbours, and many court cases have resulted from noise, smell, defecation, fornication and the territorial wanderings of pets.

In law, an animal can trespass in the same way as humans can, but the owner of a domestic cat is not responsible for the consequences of its trespass. A trespassing dog does not render its owner liable for its trespass unless in doing so it causes damage to property, game or livestock.[4] It is no

[1] For this purpose, some councils have, by local Acts of Parliament, obtained amendments to the Dogs Act 1906 (s. 3) in which such powers are available only to a police officer.

[2] D.A. 1906, s. 4, as amended by D.(A)A. 1928, s. 2.

[3] D.A. 1906, s. 3(4) as amended.

[4] A.A. 1971, s. 3.

defence that the keeper of the dog does not have control of it at the time.

A person is entitled to kill or injure a dog, if it is worrying or about to worry livestock on his land, and there is no other reasonable means of ending or preventing the worrying.[1] If a dog is killed or injured for this reason, the person doing it must give notice, within forty-eight hours, to an officer in charge of a police station.[2]

If you are attacked by a dog, you may shoot it in self defence.

A highway authority has the powers to create "designated roads" on which it is an offence to permit a dog to roam.[3] It is an offence to fail to keep the dog on a lead on such roads, and a fine may result on summary conviction. Any dog found on a highway, in breach of the designation, can be removed as a stray.

Rabies

There is an increasing risk of rabies entering Britain as a result of smuggling. The measures needed to contain an outbreak are severe and distressing.[4]

Rabies is a virus infection to which man and all warm blooded animals are susceptible. In humans it is usually fatal, and is caused by the bite of a pet, wild or stray infected animal.

The government have placed strict controls on the entry into Britain of dogs, cats and most other mammals. All must be licensed in advance, carried by authorised transport and placed in approved quarantine premises for six months.[5]

The penalties for smuggling are severe, with unlimited

---

[1] A.A. 1971, s. 9(3).

[2] A.A. 1971, s. 9(1)(b).

[3] R.T.A. 1972, s. 31(1) as amended.

[4] *Rabies is a Killer*, leaflet RL2(REV), MAFF/COI 1979.

[5] A.H.A. 1981, ss. 10, 24; Rabies (Importation of Dogs, Cats, and Other Mammals) Order, 1974. (S.I. 1974 No. 2211); Rabies (Control) Order, 1974, (S.I. 1974 No. 2212).

fines and up to one year's imprisonment, in addition to destruction of the animals.[1]

An outbreak of rabies would empower government departments and local councils to destroy foxes and other wildlife; confine with muzzling and leashing dogs, cats and other pets; seize and destroy all strays and severely restrict the movement of animals into and from an infected area.[2]

D. DANGEROUS AND FEROCIOUS ANIMALS

Licensing

If you keep a dangerous wild animal, you must have a licence issued by the local council.[3] It is an offence to keep such an animal, except in accordance with a licence, and you may be fined on summary conviction.[4]

The species of dangerous wild animal to which licensing applies, include: poisonous snakes, alligators, apes, monkeys and many larger species such as elephants and camels.[5] Licences are not required by zoos, circuses, pet shops and places registered for performing experiments.

Before granting a licence for which veterinary inspection and the payment of a fee is required, the council will need to be satisfied that:

(*a*) it is not contrary to the public interest on the grounds of safety or nuisance, **and**

(*b*) the applicant is a suitable person to hold a licence and is over the age of eighteen years, **and**

(*c*) that the animals' accommodation is escape-proof and

---

[1] A.H.A. 1981, ss. 72, 73, 74, 75, 76.

[2] A.H.A. 1981, ss. 17, 18, 19, 20. Section 13(1) gives the Minister power to make Orders, for the seizure, detention and disposal of strays, or of dogs not muzzled or kept under proper control, otherwise than in an infected area.

[1] D.W.A.A. 1976, s. 1(1).

[2] D.W.A.A. 1976, ss. 2(5), 6(1).

[3] For full list see D.W.A.A. 1976, Schd. 1, as modified and substituted by D.W.A.A. 1976 (Modification) Order, 1981, (S.I. 1981 No. 1173).

adequate in all respects for the number of animals to be kept, **and**

(*d*) the animals will be protected in case of fire or other emergency, **and**

(*e*) that all reasonable precautions will be taken to prevent and control the spread of disease, **and**

(*f*) the animal can take adequate exercise within the accommodation.[1]

You have rights of appeal against the refusal of the council to grant a licence, or any condition, variation or revocation of it.[2] The appeal is to a magistrates' court.

If a dangerous wild animal is kept without a licence or in contravention of any conditions, the council may seize, keep, destroy or otherwise dispose of it. They may recover their costs from the animal's keeper,[3] or the licence holder, and no compensation is payable.[4]

Dangerous Dogs

A magistrates' court may order you to keep a dangerous dog under proper control, or to have it destroyed.[5] A control order may be made without giving you the option of keeping it under control, even if you did not know that the dog was dangerous.

Failure to comply with a control order renders you liable to a fine on summary conviction, and the court may make a destruction order. You have a right of appeal to the Crown Court, against a destruction order but not against a control order.[6]

Depending on the seriousness of the incident, police

---

[1] D.W.A.A. 1976, s. 1(3).

[2] D.W.A.A. 1976, s. 2(1).

[3] A "keeper" is a person who has the animal in his possession, and if the animal is at large, then it is treated as being in the possession of the person who last had it in his possession.

[4] D.W.A.A. 1976, s. 4(1), (2), (3).

[5] D.A. 1871, s. 2.

[6] D.A.A. 1938, s. 1 as amended.

authorities sometimes allow a dog one "free" bite, and thereafter it may be subject to control.

Ferocious Dogs

It is an offence for any person in a street to "suffer to be at large" any unmuzzled ferocious dog, which causes obstruction, annoyance or danger to residents. It is also an offence to set on or urge any dog or other animal, to attack, worry or put in fear any person or animal.[1]

The distinction between dangerous and ferocious dogs is a matter of degree. A dog which bites small children and postmen may be dangerous but not ferocious.

Liability for injury

There are many examples of instances where you would be liable in law for injury caused by an animal under your control. You may, for example, be liable in nuisance for noise or smell from your animals, or for their trespass. Much of the civil law governing your liability for any damage caused by any animal under your control is contained in the Animals Act, 1971. The Act divides animals into dangerous and non-dangerous species.

An animal belongs to the "dangerous species" category if it is not commonly domesticated in the British Islands, and is of a type which, when fully grown, has such characteristics that it is likely, unless restrained, to cause severe damage.[2]

Whether an animal belongs to a "dangerous species" category is a question of law not fact. As a general guide, those animals described as "dangerous wild animals" in the Dangerous Wild Animals Act, 1976 (mentioned earlier) can be regarded as belonging to the "dangerous species" category of the Animals Act, 1971. For example under the 1971 Act, an elephant whether a wild jungle elephant or a trained circus elephant, is a "dangerous species".

---

[1] T.P.C.A. 1847, s. 28; P.H.A. 1875, s. 171; L.G.A. 1972, s. 180 Schd. 14, paras. 23, 26.

[2] A.A. 1971, s. 6(2).

In general terms, as a keeper of such an animal, you are liable under the Act, for any foreseeable damage (whether to persons or property) which it causes, whether or not you were negligent.

If you are the keeper of a "non-dangerous species" you are only liable for the damage it causes if:

(*a*) it was foreseeable that such damage would be caused, unless the animal was restrained,[1] **and**

(*b*) the damage was foreseeable in view of the characteristics of the animal which are not normally found in animals of that species, or are only found at particular times and in particular circumstances,[2] **and**

(*c*) you, as the keeper, knew of the "abnormal" characteristics.[3]

The present tendancy of the Courts seems to be to give the word "abnormal" generous interpretation (*i.e.* generous if you are the injured party) as the case of *Wallace v. Newton*[4] illustrates. The facts of the case were as follows:

> "A groom was severely injured in attempting to get a thoroughbred horse into its trailer. The evidence was that the horse was prone to unpredictable and unreliable behaviour. The injured groom testified that a horse like the one which injured her turns up occasionally in every stable. The court awarded damages to the groom. The 'abnormality' was the unpredictability and unreliability of the horse, and those characteristics, in themselves, rendered the horse dangerous. The injury to the groom (a broken arm leaving her with a permanent disability) was of a kind likely to be caused by a horse."

By way of further illustration, suppose that you own a domestic dog which is extremely well behaved, and has never attacked anyone. If your dog suddenly takes a fancy to your postman's leg, it is unlikely that you would be liable

---

[1] A.A. 1971, s. 2(2)(a).
[2] A.A. 1971, s. 2(2)(b).
[3] A.A. 1971, s. 2(2)(b).
[4] [1982] 1 W.L.R. 375.

("every dog is entitled to one bite"). You would however be liable, for any subsequent attack by your dog as you would then have knowledge of its characteristics.

If on application of the above rules you would be liable for damage caused by your animal (whether dangerous or otherwise) you will escape liability if you can prove:

(*a*) the damage was wholly due to the fault of the person suffering it,[1] or

(*b*) the injured person voluntarily accepted the risk,[2] or

(*c*) the injured person was a trespasser (in certain circumstances).[3]

E. PREVENTION OF CRUELTY[4]

It is an offence to beat, kick, ill-treat, override, over-drive, over-load, torture, infuriate or terrify any domestic or captive animal, and for the owner to permit such treatment.

Anyone doing so commits the offence of cruelty, and may be fined and/or imprisoned on summary conviction. Other offences include:

(*a*) transport of animals in such a way as to cause unnecessary suffering.

(*b*) procuring, assisting to procure animals, or managing premises or any place used for animal baiting or fighting.

(*c*) administering without reasonable excuse any poisonous or injurious drug.

(*d*) permitting any animal to be subjected to any operation not performed without due care and humanity.[5]

(*e*) abandoning any animal without reasonable excuse

---

[1] A.A. 1971, s. 5(1).
[2] A.A. 1971, s. 5(2).
[3] A.A. 1971, s. 5(3).
[4] See Chapter 9, para. C, p. 144 for protection of wildlife.
[5] P.A.A. 1911, s. 1(1).

permanently or not, in circumstances likely to cause unnecessary suffering.[1]

(*f*) permitting any operation to be performed on an animal without a properly administered anaesthetic.[2]

The courts may deprive a convicted owner of the animal, or order its destruction, if it would be cruel to try to keep it alive.

A police constable may arrest, without warrant,[3] any person he sees committing an offence under these provisions, or on finding a diseased or injured animal he may arrange for its destruction, in certain circumstances.[4]

Where a person has been convicted of cruelty to a dog, the court may disqualify him from keeping a dog for such period as it thinks fit.[5]

Appeals against any conviction or order of a magistrates' court, may be made to the Crown Court,[6] except against a destruction order.

---

[1] A.A.A. 1960, s. 1.
[2] P.A.(A)A. 1954, s. 1 as amended.
[3] P.A.A. 1911, s. 12.
[4] P.A.A. 1911, s. 11.
[5] P.A.(CD)A. 1933, s. 1.
[6] P.A.A. 1911, s. 14(1).

CHAPTER 9

PESTS

A. VERMINOUS PREMISES

The local council will serve notice on you as owner or occupier, if they are satisfied that your premises are:

(*a*) in such a filthy or unwholesome condition as to be prejudicial to health, or

(*b*) verminous.[1]

The notice may require the cleansing, disinfecting or whitewashing of your premises, in addition to the removal of wallpaper, and any other necessary works in order to destroy vermin. You may also be required by notice to paper, paint or distemper your house, shop or office.

The local council have the power to do the work themselves, if you fail to comply, and recover their cost from you as a civil debt.

"**vermin**" in relation to insects and parasites includes their eggs, lavae and pupae, and "verminous" is construed accordingly.[2]

If the local council require you to leave the premises during fumigation, they must provide you with alternative

---

[1] P.H.A. 1936, s. 83 as amended by P.H.A. 1961, s. 35.
[2] P.H.A. 1936, s. 90.

accommodation free of charge, and they may pay the costs of removal themselves,[1] but only if gas is used.[2]

Articles

With regard to verminous articles on your premises the council have the power to cleanse, purify, disinfect or destroy and remove any such article, at their expense. Before doing so the local council must receive certification from their officers that any such article on any premises:

(*a*) is in so filthy a condition as to render its cleanliness, purification or destruction necessary in order to prevent injury or danger of injury to the health of any person in the premises, or

(*b*) is verminous, or by reason of its having been used by, or having been in contact with any verminous person, is likely to be verminous.[3]

It is an offence for you as a dealer to sell any verminous article.[4]

Land

As the occupier of land, you are required to give notice to the local council of any infestation by rats or mice "in substantial numbers".[5] Failure to do so renders you liable to a fine on summary conviction.

If the local council becomes aware of such an infestation, either by notice from the occupier or as a result of information in their possession, they may serve you or the owner with a notice requiring specified treatment to be carried out, together with any structural works necessary.[6]

The notice will specify the period during which the treat-

[1] P.H.A. 1961, s. 36.
[2] P.H.A. 1936, s. 83(3).
[3] P.H.A. 1936, s. 84.
[4] P.H.A. 1961, s. 37.
[5] P.D.P.A. 1949, s. 3.
[6] P.D.P.A. 1949, s. 4(1)(2).

ment is to be executed, and the magistrates' court may order an occupier to give access to an owner where required.[1]

You may appeal against service of notice under the provisions of the Public Health Acts.[2]

Subject to any appeal, the council may carry out the works themselves, if you default, and recover their expenses "reasonably incurred". In addition you may be fined on summary conviction, for failing to comply with the notice.[3]

Pest Control

All local councils have a duty to keep their district free from rats and mice, but they are only obliged to treat their own land or land which they occupy. Their duties extend to enforcement of the provisions mentioned earlier in this paragraph, with regard to other owners and occupiers.[4]

In practice, most councils have for many years provided a rate-borne pest control service in respect of rats, mice, and insect pests of public health significance.[5] They can, and do make a charge for treating insect pests which are not known disease carriers.[6]

B. VERMINOUS PERSONS

Verminous persons may, either on application, by consent or by order of the magistrates' court, be removed to a cleansing station.[7]

The local council may take any necessary measures to free such a person and his clothing from vermin. If the removal results from the granting of an order of the court, then the person may be detained for such a period, and subject to such conditions as are specified in it.[8]

---

[1] P.D.P.A. 1949, s. 4(4).
[2] See Chapter 5, para. A, p. 79.
[3] P.D.P.A. 1949, s. 5.
[4] P.D.P.A. 1949, s. 2(1).
[5] *e.g.* fleas, bed bugs, cockroaches.
[6] *e.g.* ants, silverfish.
[7] P.H.A. 1936, s. 85.
[8] P.H.A. 1936, s. 85(2).

The cleansing of females may only be carried out by a registered medical practitioner, or by a woman authorised by the District Community Physician. Any consent required by the Act, for the cleansing of persons under sixteen, may be given by the parent or guardian.[1]

No charges are made for removing persons to cleansing stations, or for their detention or treatment.[2]

Examination in Schools

A local education authority[3] may by written directions to schools, authorise their medical officer to examine pupils and their clothing, in the interests of cleanliness.[4]

Any pupil found to be infested with vermin, or in a foul condition may be examined, and the parent required by notice to have the person and his clothing cleaned.[5] The notice should give at least twenty-four hours for such cleaning, in default of which the medical officer may issue an order directing the cleaning of the pupil and his clothing.

Where an order is not complied with, any authorised officer of the authority may have the pupil cleaned, and for that purpose remove and detain him, at a place provided for the purpose.[6] No female pupil may be cleaned except by a registered medical practitioner or by a woman authorised by the local education authority.

The parent of a pupil may be fined, on summary conviction if, after being cleaned under these provisions, the pupil is again found to be infested with vermin or in a foul condition, due to neglect.[7]

Pupils may be excluded from school when found in this condition, where the medical officer considers it necessary in the interest of the pupil or of other pupils.

---

[1] P.H.A. 1936, s. 85(4)(5).
[2] P.H.A. 1936, s. 85(6).
[3] County, Metropolitan District or London Borough Councils.
[4] E.A. 1944, s. 54.
[5] E.A. 1944, s. 54(2).
[6] E.A. 1944, s. 54(5).
[7] E.A. 1944, s. 54(6).

C. PROTECTION OF WILDLIFE

You may commit a variety of offences in the killing or injuring of species which are protected by law, or by the use of illegal traps or poisons, when treating for vermin.

Protected Species

Both the householder and the local council, in the pursuit of vermin, must take reasonable steps to avoid the killing or injuring of protected species of animals, birds, insects and plants.[1] It would be a defence to prove that such killing, injuring or taking was the incidental result of a lawful operation which could not reasonably have been avoided.[2]

It is an offence to set self-locking snares, so calculated to cause the killing or bodily injury to any wild animal[3] coming into contact with it.[4] If you were prosecuted under these provisions, it would be a defence to prove that the snare was set in position for the purposes of killing or taking wild animals, which can be lawfully killed (pests) in the interests of public health, agriculture, forestry, fisheries or nature conservancy, provided that you took all reasonable precautions to prevent injury to wild animals protected by the Act.

The protected species[5] are too numerous to mention but many are to be found in your garden, or nesting in a roof space. *e.g.* badgers, bats, dormice, hedgehogs, shrews and red squirrels. Protected birds include buntings, most birds of prey including the barn owl, tits, warblers and sandpipers.[5]

Most species of bat are protected, and you would commit offences in attempting to poison, trap or deny them their selected roosting places. It is an offence to damage, destroy or obstruct access to any place which a bat uses for shelter or protection. The only exception to these rules, is where bats are found in your home.[6]

---

[1] W.C.A. 1981, ss. 1, 9, 13.
[2] W.C.A. 1981, ss. 4, 10, 13.
[3] W.C.A. 1981, Schd. 6 defines the species to which this provision relates.
[4] W.C.A. 1981, s. 11.
[5] W.C.A. 1981, Schds. 1, 5, 6, for full lists.
[6] W.C.A. 1981, ss. 9–11, and 16–27.

If your bats are unwanted, you should obtain advice from the Nature Conservancy Council.[1]

Illegal Traps

You may committ offences by using spring traps (other than "approved" spring traps) for killing or taking animals,[2] or permitting the unlawful use of, or possessing, spring traps, which are to be unlawfully used.[3]

Approved spring traps include; spring traps known as break-back traps, commonly used to destroy rats, mice and other small ground vermin, including moles.[4]

You may also use spring traps of the approved type for the killing or taking of rabbits and hares, provided the traps are set in rabbit holes. Such traps must be inspected at least once daily by competent persons, between sunrise and sunset.[5] Traps may be set above ground for the killing or taking of rabbits, if done in accordance with regulations or orders for rabbit clearance, issued by the Minister of Agriculture.[6]

Illegal Poisons

Certain rodenticides have been banned by law, and those in use must kill without causing any apparent symptoms of suffering. The use of yellow phosphorus and red squill is illegal, and strychnine may only be used for the destruction of moles.[7]

---

[1] For address of the Regional Office, see local telephone directory. Further information in "*Focus on Bats—Their Conservation and the Law*" Nature Conservancy Council, 1982.

[2] "Animals" generally, means all creatures not belonging to the human race.

[3] P.A. 1954, s. 8.

[4] Small Ground Vermin Traps Order, 1958. (S.I. 1958, No. 24)

[5] P.A.A. 1911, s. 10.

[6] P.A. 1954, s. 1(1).

[7] Animals (Cruel Poisons) Act, 1962, ss. 1, 2; Animals (Cruel Poisons) Regulations, 1963, (S.I. 1963, No. 1278)

D. PLANT PESTS

Weeds

If your garden is affected by spear thistle, creeping or field thistle, curled dock, broad leaved dock or ragwort, the Minister of Agriculture may serve notice requiring you, within a specified period, to prevent them from spreading.[1]

The action is taken against the occupier, who may be prosecuted and fined if he unreasonably fails to comply with the notice.[2] The Minister has powers, in the form of his authorised officers, to carry out the work if you default, and recover the reasonable cost of so doing.

Any person authorised by the Minister[3] may enter and inspect your land for the purposes of these provisions provided that you are given notice beforehand of the intended entry. Obstruction of an authorised officer constitutes an offence.

Amenity

Under planning provisions[4] the local council may serve notice on both the owner and occupier of land, if they consider that the amenity of their area is seriously injured by its condition. The notice will specify the works required and the period during which the necessary action is to be taken.

The council are given default powers, where you fail to comply, and they may recover from the owner any reasonable expenses they incur in executing the works.[5] If the occupier is responsible for the land, the owner may in turn recover his expenses from him.

Failure to comply with the notice also renders you liable to a fine on summary conviction.[6]

---

[1] W.A. 1959, s. 1(1).
[2] W.A. 1959, s. 2(1)(2).
[3] Usually officers of a county council.
[4] T.C.P.A. 1971, s. 65.
[5] T.C.P.A. 1971, s. 107(1).
[6] T.C.P.A. 1971, s. 104(2).

You may appeal against the requirements of such a notice, to a magistrates' court, under specified circumstances.[1] The court may allow or disallow the appeal or vary the terms of the notice, and either party, if aggrieved by the decision, may appeal to the Crown Court.[2]

Colorado Beetle, etc.

Regulations have been made by the Minister of Agriculture[3] for the control of the spread of "non-indigenous plant pests"[4] which includes a wide variety of flies, beetles and moths, the most well known being the Colorado Beetle.

Any occupier who has reason to suspect that one of the specified pests[5] is on his land, must give notice immediately, in writing to the Minister. You would commit an offence by failing to give such notification or by obstructing an officer authorised by him.

---

[1] T.C.P.A. 1971, s. 105.
[2] T.C.P.A. 1971, s. 106.
[3] Plant Pests (Great Britain) Order 1980, (S.I. 1980 No. 499).
[4] Plant pests not established in Great Britain.
[5] Listed in the Import and Export (Plant Health) (Great Britain) Order, 1980, (S.I. 1980 No. 420) and the Plant Pests (Great Britain) Order, 1980, (S.I. 1980 No. 499)..

CHAPTER 10

ABUSE OF PUBLIC SERVICES

A. DRAINAGE

You may not empty into any public sewer, drain or private sewer connecting with a public sewer, any:

(*a*) matter likely to injure the sewer or drain, or interfere with the flow, or affect prejudicially the treatment and disposal of its contents.

(*b*) chemical refuse, steam or liquid at a temperature higher than 110°F (43.3°C), if it is dangerous, prejudicial to health or a nuisance.

(*c*) petroleum spirit[1] or carbide of calcium.

The penalty is a fine on summary conviction, together with a daily penalty if the offence continues, or imprisonment on conviction on indictment.[2]

If you throw or deposit any ash, cinders, bricks, stone, rubbish, dust or filth into any river, stream or watercourse, you may also be fined on summary conviction.[3]

The construction or alteration of any drains or sewers on your land, requires the approval of the local council,[4] and

---

[1] Includes oil made from petroleum or from coal. *e.g.* motor car engine oil.
[2] P.H.A. 1936, s. 2, as amended by C.P.A. 1974, s. 99 and Schd. 2.
[3] P.H.A. 1936, s. 259, to be repealed by (C.P.A. 1974, Schd. 4, when in force).
[4] Under the Building Regulations 1976. See also Chapter 11, p. 162.

you may be prosecuted and/or required to reinstate the drainage system to its original condition, where you fail to obtain such approval.[1]

Drainage includes roof drainage,[2] and any extension or alteration carried out by you, which allows excess water to fall onto your neighbours' land, may result in service of notice on you by the local council, to provide proper drainage.[3]

You may not connect any foul water drainage to the highway authority's surface water sewer. If you alter, obstruct or interfere with the authority's drain or sewer without permission, you may be guilty of an offence, and liable to a fine on summary conviction.[4] The authority have the power to carry out repair works or reinstatement and recover from you any expenses reasonably incurred.

B. ELECTRICITY

Fraudulent use and Damage

If you dishonestly use, waste or divert electricity without permission of the Electricity Board, you will be liable on conviction to a fine or imprisonment.[5] If you damage any primary meter, you would also commit an offence.[6]

You will be guilty of an offence if you unlawfully or maliciously injure any electric line or work, with the intent to cut off the supply of electricity.[7] It is also illegal to make a connection to a gas main (or electricity power main) without the consent of the undertaker[8] as well as using, fraudulently, any gas (or electricity). The undertaker would

---

[1] P.H.A. 1936, s. 65: or to effect such works to ensure compliance with the regulations.
[2] P.H.A. 1936, s. 37.
[3] P.H.A. 1936, s. 39.
[4] H.W.A. 1980, s. 100.
[5] T.A. 1968, s. 13.
[6] Electricity Supply Regulations, 1937.
[7] E.L.A. 1882, s. 22.
[8] Gas Region; Electricity Board.

be entitled to terminate the supply, irrespective of any contract which you may have entered into for supply.[1]

If you wilfully damage, remove or destroy any pipe, pillar, post, plug or lamp for the supply of gas (or electricity) you are liable to pay a fine to the undertakers, in addition to the cost of putting right the result of such damage.[2]

If you should carelessly or accidentally break, throw down or damage any pipe, pillar or lamp belonging to them, you are still liable to compensate the undertaker.[3]

Conditions of Supply

You are responsible for ensuring that your installation complies with the Regulations,[4] and for preventing any person from interfering with the Boards' apparatus.

Before carrying out any alteration or changing the use of your premises, you should give written notice to the Board. Before connecting a supply to a house or extension, the connection charges and Test Notice, must be received by the Board.

You are responsible for providing free of charge, facilities for the Board to install electricity lines to serve your property, or to run electricity lines across your property to serve a neighbour.

It is your responsibility to ensure that adequate arrangements are provided and maintained for earthing. Earthing terminals are usually provided by the Electricity Board in new property, as the traditional earthing to water mains can no longer be relied upon, due to the replacement of metal water pipes with plastic ones.

Where a coin operated prepayment meter is installed, you are responsible for the safe keeping of all coins placed

[1] G.C.A. 1847, s. 18. Sections 18, 19 and 20 of this Act were incorporated in the law relating to electricity by s. 12 E.L.A. 1882, and the E.L.(C)A. 1899. They are still in force, and where the word "gas" appears it is construed as including electricity.

[2] G.C.A. 1847, s. 19.

[3] G.C.A. 1847, s. 20.

[4] Electricity Supply Regulations, 1937.

in it, until collected by the Board, or in the case of a secondary meter, by the landlord.

One clear working day's notice must be given to the Electricity Board, of your intention to vacate premises receiving a supply of electricity.[1] Failure to do this may render you liable for the next three months consumption.

Disconnection

The Electricity Board are entitled to terminate the supply if charges are not paid by the relevant date. If disconnected for this reason, your supply will not be restored until all outstanding sums are paid, together with a fee to cover the cost of disconnection and reconnection. The Board may require, in addition a deposit as security for further sums which will become due.

C. MISUSE OF GAS

Safety Regulations[2]

As a householder you have responsibilities for ensuring that your appliances and installation pipes are safe to use. The Regulations also place obligations on gas installers and the Gas Region.[3]

In particular, you must ensure that:

(*a*) installations are only done by competent persons.

(*b*) the air supply is adequate, so that the appliance can operate efficiently and safely.

(*c*) flueways are clear and in good working order.

(*d*) the room is properly ventilated.

(*e*) the appliance and its fittings are gas tight.

---

[1] E.L.A. 1909, s. 17.

[2] Gas Safety Regulations 1972, S.I. 1972, No. 1178. Revised Gas Safety Regulations are to be published, and are expected to include, amongst other things, requirements for the safe use of propane and butane.

[3] G.S. Regs. 1972, Part 6.

(*f*) the appliance or any gas fitting is not faulty or maladjusted resulting in danger to persons or property.[1]

Escapes of Gas

If you become aware of an escape of gas in your home, you must immediately shut off the gas supply at the appropriate place to isolate the defective appliance or part of the installation.[2]

If the gas continues to escape, you must give notice "as soon as practicable" to the Gas Region office,[3] and you must not re-open the supply until the fault has been rectified,[4] except that a brief and controlled restoration of supply by a competent person is normal to assist in leak detection.

Disconnection

If your gas supply is terminated or a gas fitting isolated for reasons of safety, the Gas Region must display on or close to the appliance or pipe, a prominent notice to that effect.[5] The notice must also state:

(*a*) your right of appeal to the Secretary of State for Energy against the action taken.

(*b*) that if you re-connect without authority you are committing an offence.

(*c*) the penalty, on summary conviction, for failing to observe the Regulations.

In addition, the Gas Region must give you, within five working days, a written notice stating:

(*a*) the reason for disconnection and the nature of any defect.

(*b*) the nature of the danger, and the action taken.

---

[1] G.S. Regs. 1972. Regulations 35(2), 45(1), 47(a) to (e).
[2] G.S. Regs. 1972, Reg. 48(1).
[3] G.S. Regs. 1972. Reg. 48(2).
[4] G.S. Regs. 1972. Reg. 48(3).
[5] Gas Safety (Rights of Entry) Regulations, 1983 (S.I. 1983, No. 1575).

(*c*) the right to appeal, within twenty-one days to the Secretary of State for Energy, against the action taken.

You cannot reconnect any gas fitting or part of a gas system, or restore the supply to premises known to be cut off for safety reasons, or connect where the Gas Region has refused to supply gas, without written consent either from them or the Secretary of State.

Where consent is given, restoration must be done by competent persons.

Fraudulent Use and Damage

If you use or deal with gas so as to interfere with the efficient supply to any consumer, the Gas Region may cease to supply you with gas.[1]

If you wilfully, fraudulently or by culpable negligence injure any pipes, meters or fittings, or alter the meter or prevent it from registering the quantity of gas supplied, you will be guilty of an offence. The penalty is a fine, on summary conviction together with a requirement to repay to the Gas Region the cost of any remedial works.[2]

Further offences relating to damage to the Gas Regions' pipes, meters and fittings, and the fraudulent use of gas, are described in the previous paragraph, in which the words "electricity" and "gas" are synonymous.[3]

D. MISUSE OF TELEPHONES

It is an offence to use the telephone or telex system with the intent of avoiding payment, and you would be liable to a fine and/or imprisonment on summary conviction.[4] Sending indecent, offensive, obscene or false telephone messages or

---

[1] G.A. 1972, Schd. 4, para. 19, as amended by G.A. 1980, s. 1.
[2] G.A. 1972, Schd. 4, para. 20, as amended.
[3] G.C.A. 1847, ss. 18, 19, 20.
[4] P.O.A. 1953, s. 65A, as amended by P.O.A. 1969 Schd. 4, to be repealed by B.T.A. 1981, Schd. 6, Part II, when in force.

telegrams, for the purposes of causing annoyance, inconvenience or needless anxiety is punishable by fine.[1]

Unsolicited Telephone Calls

You may feel that unsolicited sales calls are approaching misuse of the telephone system when frequently occurring. You may strongly resent being approached in this way, particularly if the calls are over-persistent and aggressive selling techniques are employed. The office of the Director General of Fair Trading has issued guidelines[2] in an attempt to discourage undesirable practices. The Department have also suggested a scheme, similar to the Post Office Mailing Preference Service[3] be established. This would enable Telecom customers not wishing to receive unsolicited telephone sales calls, to have their names removed from the lists used by the direct marketing firms.

E. MISUSE OF WATER

Waste

You will be guilty of an offence, as an owner or occupier, if you wilfully or negligently waste, misuse, unduly consume or contaminate water, as a result of failing to maintain water fittings.[4]

In addition, you may be required to remedy the defect within forty-eight hours, otherwise the water authority will be entitled to carry out the necessary work and recover from you the expenses reasonably incurred.[5]

Misuse

If the water authority believe that a serious deficiency of water exists, or is threatened, they may by publication of a

---

[1] P.O.A. 1969, s. 78, to be repealed by B.T.A. 1981, Schd. 6, part 2 when in force.

[2] *Telephone Selling*. March 1983. Department of Consumer Affairs.

[3] Details and application forms for the Mailing Preference Service, are obtainable from: Mailing Preference Service, Freepost 22, London W1E 7EZ.

[4] W.A. 1945, Schd. 3, para. 64, as amended by W.A. 1948, s. 11(4).

[5] As a civil debt in the county court, see Chapter 5, para. C, p. 83.

notice in two or more newspapers circulating in the area, impose a ban on, or restrict the use of hosepipes. The prohibition or restriction may apply to all or any part of the area of supply, and may prevent you from watering your garden or washing your car, by use of a hosepipe.[1]

Damage

If you wilfully or negligently injure any water fitting belonging to the water authority, you may be prosecuted and fined. The authority may also repair the damage and recover their costs from you as a civil debt.[2]

Pollution

Pollution of a spring, well, borehole or adit supplying water for human consumption is an offence, and you would be liable to a fine on summary conviction or imprisonment on indictment.[3]

Your private domestic water supply, from a well, tank or spring, may be temporarily or permanently closed by the local council.[4] The council would apply to the magistrates' court for an order requiring such closure, if they are satisfied that the supply is, or is likely to be so polluted as to be prejudicial to health. The court may, on hearing any owner or occupier, direct that the supply be used only for specific purposes,[5] of that further analysis be carried out.[6]

The local council may serve an abatement notice on you, if any well, tank, cistern or water butt is in such a state as to render any water for domestic purposes liable to contamination.[7]

---

[3] W.A. 1945, s. 16, as amended by W.A. 1948, s. 6.
[2] W.A. 1945, Schd. 3, para. 67.
[3] W.A. 1945, s. 21(1), as amended by W.R.A. 1963, Schd. 13 and C.P.A. 1974, Schd. 2.
[4] P.H.A. 1936, s. 140(1).
[5] P.H.A. 1936, s. 140(2).
[6] P.H.A. 1936, s. 140(2).
[7] P.H.A. 1936, s. 141, see also Chapter 7, para. C, p. 123.

Rejection of Plans

If the plans for your new house fail to show satisfactory provision for a wholesome supply of water sufficient for domestic purposes, the local council may reject them under the Building Regulations. You may appeal against such rejection to a magistrates' court.

If the plans are passed and you fail to put into effect any proposal for provision of a water supply, the council may serve notice on you prohibiting occupation.[1]

Liability for Rates

Your water rates are payable on demand, and should you fail to pay within seven days, the water authority may terminate the supply and recover their expenses in so doing, together with the outstanding debt, in the county court,[2] or magistrate's court.

If within those seven days, you give notice in writing to the water authority that the amount due is in dispute, or that some other person is liable to pay, they cannot terminate the supply until such dispute is settled.[3]

As an owner or occupier of a house supplied by a pipe serving two or more houses, you are liable to pay the same water rate as if supplied by a separate pipe.[4]

If the water authority have reason to believe that you intend leaving the premises, to evade payment of the water rates, they may apply to a justice of the peace for either, a summons for non-payment or a warrant to enter the premises and seize goods and chattels to the value of the debt, or both.[5]

The water authority are obliged to notify the local council within forty-eight hours, where any supply to an inhabited house is cut off by them.[6]

---

[1] P.H.A. 1936, s. 137, as amended by W.A. 1945, s. 29.
[2] W.A. 1945, s. 38, as amended by W.A. 1973 Schd. 9.
[3] By the Lands Tribunal. See Chapter 5, para. H, p. 100.
[4] W.A. 1945, Schd. 3, para. 53.
[5] W.A. 1945, Schd. 3, para. 58.
[6] W.A. 1945, s. 39, as amended.

CHAPTER 11

PROPERTY CHANGES

A. PLANNING

Before carrying out any "building, engineering, mining or other operations, in, over or under land, or making any material changes in the use of buildings or land",[1] you must apply to the local council for permission.

Development includes amongst the matters mentioned above, dividing one house into two or more dwellings. Engineering operations includes the formation or laying out of means of access to highways.[2]

Development does not include improvements or alterations which do not materially affect the external appearance of your house,[3] or reversion to a former use, in certain cases.[4]

If you are in doubt whether or not your project requires planning permission you may apply to the council for the matter to be determined.[5] This may be done by letter giving details of present and proposed uses, and works to be undertaken, and may be made at the same time as a formal application for permission.

As far as the householder is concerned, there are four types of application for planning permission:

---

[1] This is "development" T.C.P.A. 1972, s. 22.
[2] T.C.P.A. 1971, s. 290.
[3] T.C.P.A. 1971, s. 22.
[4] T.C.P.A. 1971, s. 23.
[5] T.C.P.A. 1971, s. 53.

(*a*) *Outline Planning Permission*; where you wish to know whether permission will be given for the erection of buildings on a site, before detailed drawings are prepared.

(*b*) *Approval of Reserved Matters*: where you wish to extend the period for which an outline application has been approved. Failure to reserve approved matters within the period stated on the approval, may mean that permission lapses.[1]

(*c*) *Full Planning Permission*: where you wish to carry out development or effect a change of use. You could also apply in retrospect, where development has been carried out without permission, in order to regularise the situation.

(*d*) *Renewal of Temporary Permission, or Relief from Conditional Permission*: where you wish to continue a temporary use beyond the time limit imposed, or to continue a use without complying with conditions attached to the original permission.

Applications

You should make application on the forms obtainable from your local council's Planning Department, who will normally give you notes for guidance in their completion.

Site plans should accompany your application (except for approval of reserved matters) drawn to a scale of not less than 1/2500, showing the site to which your application refers, and its boundary. The site should be edged or shaded in red, and any other "parcels" of land in your ownership shaded or edged in blue. If your house has a numbered address, in a regular sequence of numbers on a defined road, the council may not insist on a site plan.

Detailed drawings are required (except for outline applications) and should be at a scale of not less than 1/100 (metric) or ⅛ inch to 1 foot (imperial). Your drawings should show the existing features of the site, and give

[1] T.C.P.A. 1971, ss. 41, 42.

sufficient detail to provide a clear picture of any new dwelling or extension. They must clearly indicate the location of the proposed development within the site, and the amount of floor space to be used for different purposes. Any detail of an extension should be distinctly coloured, and means of access to the site, and type of wall or fence enclosing the site should be shown.

Applications for a "change of use" of part of the premises must be accompanied by floor plans, showing the extent of existing and proposed uses. Such changes would include conversion from wholly domestic to part domestic and part retail or commercial uses.

If you own the land in question, your application must be accompanied by a certificate of ownership.[1] The appropriate scale fee is also required.[2]

Applications for certain types of development (generally known as "bad neighbour developments") must first be advertised so that neighbours are given an opportunity to object.[3]

There are numerous types of such developments, and include boarding kennels, bingo halls, slaughterhouses and scrapyards. As a householder, you are more likely to be the person affected rather than the proposed developer.[4]

Local councils are obliged to keep a register of applications and the decisions made on them, which is open for public inspection.

Permitted Development

Certain types of development are regarded as being "permitted" and do not require permission.[5]

These include:

[1] T.C.P.A. 1971, s. 26.

[2] Town and Country Planning (Fees for Applications and Deemed Permissions) Regulations, 1981 and 1982 (S.I. 1981 No. 369 and 1982 No. 716).

[3] T.C.P.A. 1971, s. 26.

[4] Town and Country Planning General Development Order 1977, Article 8.

[5] Town and Country Planning General Development Orders 1977 to 1981; (S.I. 1977, No. 289; S.I. 1980, No. 1946, S.I. 1981, No. 245)

(*a*) Enlargement of dwellings where:

(*i*) the original cubic content is not exceeded by more than 50 cubic metres or 10% in the case of a terraced house, or 70 cubic metres or 15% for any other dwelling, whichever is the greater in each case, **and**

(*ii*) the total enlargement does not exceed 115 cubic metres, **and**

(*iii*) no part of the extension projects above the original house or beyond the foremost part of any wall of the house fronting onto a highway, **and**

(*iv*) no part of the extension exceeding four metres in height must lie within two metres of any boundary.

(*b*) Erection of a separate building, e.g. a garage, except that it must not be within 5 metres of your house, or exceed 4 metres in height if the roof is pitched or 3 metres if not, otherwise permission is required.

All the factors in (*a*) above also apply.

(*c*) Erection of buildings for a purpose incidental to the enjoyment of your house, e.g. the keeping of bees, poultry, pet animals etc., for the domestic needs or personal enjoyment of the occupants of the house. The conditions in (*a*) (*iii*) and (*iv*) above apply, and the building area should not exceed 50% of the area of the garden exclusive of the ground area of the house.

(*d*) A stable, subject to the conditions in (*a*) above, except that it must be **within** five metres of the house.

(*e*) Works by statutory undertakers on gas, electricity, drainage and water services.

(*f*) Greenhouses, summerhouses and sheds.

(*g*) Swimming pools, ponds, underground tanks, cesspools and septic tanks.

(*h*) Hardstandings for vehicles, provided that they are incidental to the enjoyment of the house. The formation of an access (a "crossing" over a pavement) **would** require permission.

(*i*) The construction of fences, gates and walls, provided they do not exceed one metre in height when abutting a highway, or two metres elsewhere.

(*j*) Erection of oil tanks in your garden for domestic heating oil, provided the capacity does not exceed 3500 litres (770 gallons). No part must be more than 3 metres above ground level. Condition (*a*) (*iii*) above also applies.

(*k*) Temporary buildings necessary for approved construction work.

(*l*) Maintenance and painting, provided that the maintenance does not materially affect the external appearance, and the painting is not in the form of an advertisement.

Permission

You may receive permission in two ways. First by the making of a development order by the Secretary of State, which may have the effect of granting consent for certain types of development. Secondly from the council, who might give permission unconditionally or subject to conditions which they wish to impose. The conditions must be reasonable and relate to the proposed development.

If permission is refused, or granted subject to conditions which you do not agree with, you are entitled to appeal to the Secretary of State, Department of the Environment.[1]

Deemed Refusal

If the council fail to make a decision on your application within eight weeks of the date of its submission, it is deemed

---

[1] T.C.P.A. 1971, s. 36(1) see Chapter 5, para. E, p. 92.

to have been refused. You would, in the absence of such decision, be entitled to appeal against the implied refusal.

The eight week period may be extended by written agreement with the applicant.

B. BUILDING REGULATIONS

Applications

You are required to make application to the local council, for approval (in addition to any planning approval required) to erect, extend or alter a building.[1] You should complete the forms provided by the council and submit them with plans, sections, specifications, an estimate of the work,[2] and the required fee.[3]

The form, which constitutes your "notice of intention" should be accompanied by detailed plans, drawn to a scale of not less than 1/100. Block plans should be drawn to a scale of not less than 1/1250, and key plans to a scale of not less than 1/2500. There is no requirement as in the distant past, for plans to be drawn on linen, but they must be executed or reproduced in a clear and intelligible manner, and with suitable and durable materials.

Every notice, drawing or plan must be signed by the applicant, or his agent indicating the name and address of the person on whose behalf they are submitted.

Exemptions

Some buildings will be wholly exempt and others partially exempt in that only some of the Regulations' requirements need be complied with.

Wholly exempt buildings include: single storey huts, sheds, shelters and kiosks, not exceeding 9 square metres in area, and not containing a water closet, or constructed of combustible material, or not within two metres of a

---

[1] P.H.A. 1936, s. 61(1).
[2] Building Regulations 1976, (S.I. 1976 No. 1676) Reg. A10(1), Schd. 3.
[3] Building (Prescribed Fees) Regulations, 1982. (S.I. 1982, No. 577)

building, or erected over a public sewer. Others include: tents, marquees, caravans, tower masts not attached to a building, scaffolding, fences, walls and gates not part of a building, storage tanks not being septic tanks, settlement tanks, cesspools or tower silos.[1]

Partially exempt buildings[2] include: summer houses, poultry houses, aviaries, greenhouses, conservatories, orchard houses, boathouses, coalsheds, garden tool sheds and cycle sheds. You must still, however, submit an application for approval.

Relaxations

If you wish, for example, to fill your cavity walls with insulating material, it is necessary to submit an application for relaxation of the Regulations.[3] The relaxation will only be given for the installation of approved cavity fill materials.

Relaxations may be given for other matters: preservation of zones of open space;[4] structural fire precautions in external walls;[5] thermal insulation values of walls, floors and roofs.[6] etc.

Passing of Plans

The council may pass or reject your plans, and inspect any work to see that it conforms to the Regulations.[7] Contravention of the Regulations is punishable by fine on summary conviction[8] and the council may require the removal or alteration of any works which do not meet the requirements.[9]

---

[1] Building Regulations 1976, Reg. A5(1).
[2] Building Regulations 1976, Reg. A5(2)(a), Schd 2, Part A.
[3] Building Regulations 1976, Reg. C9(2).
[4] Regulation K3(1).
[5] Regulation E7.
[6] Regulation F3.
[7] P.H.A. 1936, ss. 64, 287(1)(a) as amended by H.S.W.A. 1974, s. 63.
[8] P.H.A. 1961, s. 4(6) as amended by H.S.W.A. 1974, Schds. 6 and 10.
[9] P.H.A. 1936, s. 65.

Appeals

In the event of a dispute between you and the council on any matter concerning defective plans or contraventions of the regulations, such matters can be determined by a magistrates' court. Alternatively if both parties agree, the dispute may be referred to the Secretary of State, Department of the Environment, for settlement.

Either party may appeal to the High Court on any question of law.[1]

Approval

The council are under a statutory obligation to give you notice of the passing or rejection of your plans within five weeks of their submission. The period may be extended to two months, with your written consent.[2]

Where no approval or rejection is given within such period, there is nothing to prevent you from going ahead with the work, though you would risk prosecution if you contravene the regulations.[3]

Inspections

The council's building inspectors may make inspections during the progress of site works, at various stages, e.g. when foundations, damp-proof course or drainage works, etc., are complete.

Two legal cases, heard in the 1970's, have posed burdens of responsibility for these inspections on all councils.

In one case, where a building inspector had inspected foundation works which subsequently failed, resulting in damage, the council were held liable for his negligent inspection.[4] In the second case, foundations were not constructed in accordance with the submitted plans. The council were held liable for subsequent damage where no inspection had

---

[1] P.H.A. 1936, ss. 64, 67 as amended by P.H.A. 1961, Schd. 1 and H.S.W.A. 1974.

[2] P.H.A. 1936, s. 64, as amended by P.H.A. 1961, s. 10(2).

[3] P.H.A. 1961, s. 4(6).

[4] *Dutton v. Bognor Regis Urban District Council* [1972] 1 All E.R. 462.

been carried out, and the absence of such inspection could not be justified.[1]

FINIS

There are rights after death.

If at the end of this life, you die without leaving any funds, saleable assets or traceable relatives, the local council will arrange for your disposal, at their expense.[2]

If you die in these circumstances in hospital, the council, not the hospital authority, have a duty to have you buried,[3] but not cremated if it was known to be against your wishes.

---

[1] *Anns v. London Borough of Merton* [1977] 2 All E.R. 492.
[2] N.A.A. 1948, s. 50(1).
[3] *Secretary of State for Scotland v. Fife County Council* [1953] S.C. 257.

Table of Cases

Alphabetical Index

A

B

C

E

F

G

K

L

O

P

Q

R

S

T

U

PRINTED IN GREAT BRITAIN BY
The Eastern Press Limited
SPECIALIST LAW BOOK
AND JOURNAL PRINTERS
LONDON AND READING